"I know this guy. With my own two eyes, I've watched God prepare BJ Thompson, equip him, raise him up, and use him remarkably to help people thrive. What I've had the privilege to receive from this gifted author in bits and pieces across restaurant tables, through phone conversations, and text exchanges, you now get to glean in full through this book. BJ Thompson lives what he preaches. And we might just live a little longer for having listened."

—BETH MOORE, Living Proof Ministries

"In *Awaken a Better You*, BJ Thompson masterfully shows us how it is possible to experience transformation in every realm of life. He tells us that we can be all that God created us to be and shows us how. This book contains the wisdom and practical steps necessary to tr___ thrive in life. No matter where you are on your life's jo___ _____ ___ _etter You will help you reach the next level."

—CHRISTINE_____en

"I've known BJ Thompson for m_____ ___n a consistent voice in my life. His wisd_____ _anding of people and human behavior can really only be c___gorized as a gift. BJ has a unique ability to synthesize large ideas into simple and applicable ways that I've never seen before. He is committed to his own growth and development, alongside helping others on their transformational journey. He cares for himself and his friends in a way that makes *Awaken a Better You* another extension of what he already does for so many."

—ANDY MINEO, recording artist

"*Awaken a Better You* is the book we need today and tomorrow. With the world feeling like it's on fire, we all need to take deep breaths, pause, and know that we are truly loved even in our messiness. BJ Thompson delivers the hope we need in this book. To create a better world, we must create a better us. It's a reminder as we toil to remember ourselves and our creator who loves us deeply. This book is the beginning steps to transformation and holy inspiration."

—LATASHA MORRISON, founder and president of Be the Bridge

"There are so many individuals that take on the expert title without having paid the price, but BJ Thompson has done the work. You can trust his voice and wisdom in the areas he has in fact lived."

—SAM COLLIER, lead pastor of Story Church Atlanta and
founder of A Greater Story Ministries

"BJ Thompson has written a must-read book for anyone tired of waiting for their life to start. His own story will give you confidence to believe that you are more than what has happened to you. It's time to *Awaken a Better You* in ways you didn't think were possible."

—HEATHER THOMPSON DAY, author of *I'll See You Tomorrow*

"BJ draws from his own real-life experiences to guide readers toward a better life. I feel like I'm being advised by a close friend. Each lesson is concise, memorable, and actionable. I recommend *Awaken a Better You* to anybody who is looking to grow into a more aligned version of themself."

—MICHELL CLARK, author of *Keep It 100* and co-founder
of *The Creative Summer Company*

"Everyone wants to build a better version of themselves, but years of discarded New Year's resolutions testify to the difficulty of that task. In *Awaken a Better You,* BJ Thompson compresses more than two decades of experience as a life coach into a volume filled with practical wisdom and riveting real-life stories. This is the kind of book that makes you believe not only that change is possible but that it's possible for *you*."

—JEMAR TISBY, PHD, *New York Times* bestselling author of *The Color of Compromise* and *How to Fight Racism*

"BJ is committed to the holistic health of everyone he encounters. He understands that before we can have a better community, we must be better people. *Awaken a Better You* challenges us to be our best selves and gives us practical steps to do so."

—LISA V. FIELDS, founder and president of Jude 3 Project

"*Awaken a Better You* was an absolute mindset shift for me. If you're feeling stuck and can't seem to access that next gear, this is the book for you. BJ Thompson is the guide I wish I had two decades ago because he cares about all of you—your mind, body, spirit, emotions, and relationships. This book will help you unlock your potential, change adversity into opportunity, and embody who you were always created to be."

—STEVE CARTER, pastor and author of *The Thing Beneath the Thing*

"BJ is a once-in-a-lifetime type of person. His care for others' well-being shines through every page of this book."

—PROPAGANDA, artist, poet, and author of the Nautilus Silver Award–winning book *Terraform: Building a Better World*

"Speaking with conviction and wisdom that was forged through lived experience, BJ Thompson breaks down the complexity of positive transformation into simple and applicable action steps."

—KYLE KORVER, seventeen-year NBA veteran

Awaken a Better You

Awaken a Better You

4 SIMPLE STEPS TO CREATE THE LIFE YOU WANT

BJ Thompson

WATERBROOK

Scripture quotations, unless otherwise indicated, are taken from the ESV® Bible (The Holy Bible, English Standard Version®), copyright © 2001 by Crossway, a publishing ministry of Good News Publishers. Used by permission. All rights reserved. Scripture quotations marked (KJV) are taken from the King James Version.

Details in some anecdotes and stories have been changed to protect the identities of the persons involved.

Copyright © 2023 by BJ Thompson
Foreword by Lecrae Moore copyright © 2023 by Penguin Random House LLC

All rights reserved.

Published in the United States by WaterBrook, an imprint of Random House, a division of Penguin Random House LLC.

WaterBrook® and its deer colophon are registered trademarks of Penguin Random House LLC.

Trade Paperback ISBN 978-0-593-19421-8
Ebook ISBN 978-0-593-19422-5

Library of Congress Cataloging-in-Publication Data
Names: Thompson, BJ (Life Coach), author.
Title: Awaken a better you : 4 simple steps to create the life you want / BJ Thompson.
Description: First edition. | Colorado Springs : WaterBrook, [2023] |
Includes bibliographical references.
Identifiers: LCCN 2022017256 | ISBN 9780593194218 (trade paperback) |
ISBN 9780593194225 (ebook)
Subjects: LCSH: Change (Psychology)—Religious aspects—Christianity. | Success—Religious aspects—Christianity.
Classification: LCC BV4599.5.C44 T46 2023 | DDC 204/.4—dc23/eng/20220805
LC record available at https://lccn.loc.gov/2022017256

Printed in the United States of America on acid-free paper

waterbrookmultnomah.com

2 4 6 8 9 7 5 3 1

First Edition

Book design by Caroline Cunningham

Special Sales Most WaterBrook books are available at special quantity discounts when purchased in bulk by corporations, organizations, and special-interest groups. Custom imprinting or excerpting can also be done to fit special needs. For information, please email specialmarketscms@penguinrandomhouse.com.

This book is dedicated to my father,

Ronnie Joe Thompson,

who taught me by example that the greatest power

in life is helping others become strong.

Foreword

As a twenty-year-old in college, I had a very powerful spiritual transformation. I made a commitment to no more drugs and no more alcohol abuse and decided to focus on a healthy lifestyle. But I didn't want to hide it. Instead, I was vocal around campus about changing my habits.

Yet two years passed, and I was in a slump. I had come from a broken home, was struggling with my faith, and didn't have any real friends. I was depressed and looking for my identity in a relationship. I was on an island, trying to figure out life.

One day, I wandered into the campus gym—thin and insecure, but trying to bulk up to impress the ladies. A young man, roughly my age, walked into the gym. He was vibrant, verbose, and muscular. He stared at me for a second, then walked over to me and said, "Aren't you Lecrae? Aren't you the guy who changed his life?"

I felt exposed. I thought I was hiding in the shadows and that no one remembered the promises I had made to myself and others. I thought maybe I could fade into obscurity, but this guy was shining a light on me. I acknowledged I was who he thought I was and then tried to move past it.

This guy wouldn't let up though. He inquired about what I was up to and what my life looked like. At first, his intentionality disturbed me. His intrusion into my space made me dislike him. Yet that moment would change everything. I left that day challenged and convicted to be who I believed I was created to be.

The young man who approached me was BJ Thompson. He would later become one of the most pivotal people in my life. Even as a younger, less-informed man, BJ was still leaving an indelible mark on people. Through his passion and intentionality, I became a better me.

I count you, dear reader, as blessed because BJ has now accumulated years of wisdom, insight, and experience that he will pass on to you through this book. I've seen him weather storms of death, division, and despair. He's been to the farthest corners of the world and walked people off the edge of hopelessness. This book is the accumulation of those experiences, brought to you.

Many people will offer segmented approaches to health and choose only one part to address: relational, emotional, mental, physical, spiritual. However, BJ has learned that those areas are integrated and should be treated as such. A better you does not mean simply a better mind, marriage, career, or parent. Rather, a better you means all those areas of your life will be influenced because you dealt with yourself as a whole.

Your life is a story and, like me, you may have had some pretty bad chapters. But it's time to turn the page and write some stories of growth, transformation, and change. The journey begins now.

—Lecrae

Contents

FOREWORD BY LECRAE   ix

PART ONE: Start Here   1

1 HIGH RISK, HIGH REWARD   15

2 THE VALUE OF YOU   23

3 ON THE RED CARPET   39

4 BEWARE THE WIZ   49

PART TWO: How to Build a Better You   65

5 AWAKEN A BETTER MENTAL AND EMOTIONAL YOU   76

6 AWAKEN A BETTER PHYSICAL YOU   99

7 AWAKEN A BETTER RELATIONAL YOU   122

8 AWAKEN A BETTER SPIRITUAL YOU   156

CONCLUSION: A BETTER YOU   177

ACKNOWLEDGMENTS   183

NOTES   187

PART ONE

Start Here

shouldn't even be here. By rights, I should be dead. I shouldn't be anything close to successful.

I was a premature baby, birthed to a seventeen-year-old mother and a father who left school in the tenth grade. I was raised in two zip codes that had the highest incarceration rates in Texas during the height of gang culture. John Singleton's movie *Boyz n the Hood* was more than a window into my world—it was my life.

I spent my early years as a latchkey kid, caring for my two younger siblings, convinced it was my job to keep us all alive. From a very young age, I recognized that though I loved my family, our life together was harder than it needed to be. I remember walking to the kitchen for cereal, turning the lights on, and watching as roaches scattered like a party had just ended. While we hoped there wasn't one in the box, if roaches did get in the cereal, we would act like they were raisins—if you know, you know. I didn't yet have the words to describe our poverty-stricken lifestyle, but it felt like something was working against us. Everything was hard.

SURVIVAL

When I was seven, my family went to a concert where a fight broke out and led to a shoot-out—the first of many in my young life. At eleven, I was jumped for the first time by a gang of eight kids. Later that year, I was in my first drive-by shooting. At sixteen, I experienced my first stampede riot. The week after graduating from a school with the most gang-affiliated students in South Dallas, I almost died in a shoot-out on the freeway.

Things weren't just dangerous on the streets, though. They could be just as serious at home. One day, I got a strange call asking for the whereabouts of one of my relatives, and I said, "He's in the back. Who is this?" Next thing I knew, there was a loud bang at the door and someone was screaming, "Open up, police!" I looked up as officers rushed into my house to pick up my relative for drugs or a related violation. I was speechless. Watching them carry away a close connection was unsettling and disturbing. If that was his future, was it also mine?

THE ODDS WERE STACKED AGAINST ME

Making it more difficult, I came of age in a nation that has a four-hundred-year history of creating racially biased systems and enslaving and degrading people of color. I experienced the generational fallout of this dynamic firsthand. Those of you raised in similar circumstances can join me in testifying. We were in no way well positioned to succeed.

Like me, maybe you grew up not knowing a single person who worked a white-collar job, mostly because the White people took those sorts of jobs with them in what sociologists term *white flight*.[1] Not a doctor, not a lawyer, not a business owner was left—unless you count the "street pharmacists" on the corners.

Growing up in a hardworking, blue-collar community alongside a neighborhood Crip gang, none of us could imagine anything different. At best, we would become rappers, sell drugs, or go to the league. If you were really talented, you'd get a job in a call center and make just enough to live in a loft downtown. That was the future laid out for me.

Yet here I am. A walking miracle. Beyond simply making it

out alive, I've become a global leader—an author, speaker, and life coach with more than twenty years of experience. As the founder and executive director of the growth and development organization Build a Better Us, I've coached tens of thousands of people—including professional athletes, entertainers, and global influencers—toward transformation. I also helped launch the 116 Movement, a faith movement that has influenced millions of people around the world.

How did I get here? How did I overcome the barriers before me so I could "make it"? My journey wasn't some huge leap. I'm no different from you. I feel just as much fear at the idea of change. I try new things and make mistakes and fail and have to try again. But I made a decision at a very early age that I would not simply go with the flow of my surroundings. Instead, I would take hold of my agency—my power to choose.

HARSH BEGINNINGS

Before the start of third grade, my parents had saved up enough money to buy us a spacious home in Pleasant Grove, and I was transferred to a new school. The only problem, I didn't know a single soul, and it seemed like trouble sought me out every chance it got. Once, I was chased home by a group of kids. Another time, I was walking home from school and suddenly felt a fist hit the back of my head. I was jumped by eight to ten boys for simply breathing the wrong way. And to top it off, my shoes were from Payless in the era when everyone wore Jordans and name-brand shoes. I was roasted almost every day. "That ain't Jordan. That's an overweight man leaning on a backboard." I hated school.

I wanted to fit in and be a happy kid, but I found myself socially rejected and ducking bullies daily. They would see me in the hall, dart in my direction, and push me, mock me, or do something else that shook me. I was a little, scrawny kid trying to survive, and in doing so, I was allowing my life to just happen.

THE MOMENT EVERYTHING CHANGED

On the last day of school, my classmates were all hanging over one another, crying. We were all transitioning from elementary school to middle school, and everything would change. Friend groups would be split up, sent to different places. They all loved one another so much. And there I was, watching them carry on while I sat at my desk by myself.

Nobody cared where I was going. Nobody cared what would happen to me. Nobody cared, period. I might as well have been invisible. I had been there for several years. I ate lunch and played games with these kids. I had suffered abuse from them. Hadn't I done enough to be missed? Not even one person was sad I was leaving? That's when it dawned on me. Letting life just happen, letting it all wash over me, had led to full rejection. Sitting there alone, my face flooded in tears, I felt the ground shift beneath my feet.

I would never make this mistake again. Never again would I let life just happen. From that moment on, I would dictate how my life would go. I would define my own identity and become the social influencer in my environment. I would be a leader, not a follower.

In that moment of desperation, I took the first baby steps on my journey toward transformation. Over the course of my life, I would experience transforming faith, restored relationships, emotional healing, trauma recovery—in short, total transformation. It wasn't a huge leap but a series of smaller steps that led to progress. And it all began from a place of desperation.

Perhaps you can relate. You're hunting for growth, hungry for change. In order to take your first steps, you'll have to make a choice like sixth-grade me did. From the depths of desperation, you must come to a decision. You couldn't control where you started, but you can choose where you go. You can

> **It all starts with deciding that you want to change.**

learn how to grow in mind, body, and spirit—learn how to foster healthy relationships that propel you instead of hold you back. Your past does not have to dictate your future. It all starts with deciding that you want to change and that you won't allow anything to hold you back—not even you.

MANUAL MODE

Reject the idea that a great God made you to be mediocre. You have been made with purpose. Growing your potential into your purpose is not magical, though. My transformation into a better me didn't happen overnight, and yours won't either. It will be a progression. No one can become a better version of themselves out of nowhere. There is no autopilot function that will result in awakening a better you. Instead, you will have to step into the sometimes-uncomfortable process of knowing who you are.

That means being honest about your entire story—good, bad, and ugly—not simply the chapter of life that you are most proud of. Read that again. Unfortunately, some people try to skip a rung in that ladder. Bypassing self-reflection and personal development, they try to take the helm before they've studied how to sail a boat. The next thing they know, they've run onto the rocks and are taking on water. They're sinking fast and feel they have no choice but to abandon ship. Don't let that happen to you. Before you can become a better version of yourself, you must discover and own who you are and appreciate the richness and value in your entire story. You must mine the depths of who God has truly created you to be. To do so, let's go back to the basics.

YOU ARE DEEPLY LOVED

Every thought in this book—and the basis of who you are—is undergirded by one basic principle: You are a mess—yet deeply loved by God. Reread that last statement. You are a mess—yet deeply loved by God. No amount of personal development will make you any more worthy than God already finds you. You're already loved. Just as you are.

Hear me. The ultimate goal of this book is not to change who you are. God has already empowered you with everything you need to become the best version of yourself. Instead, I aim to provide the resources by which you can unlock greater mental, spiritual, relational, and emotional health by moving through four growth points: from desperation to information to application to transformation. In doing so, you can achieve the sort of balanced, holistic health—involving mind, body, and spirit—that can awaken the better you that God intends you to be.

> You are a mess—
> yet deeply loved by God.

While I wrote this book from a Judeo-Christian worldview, the principles will work for anyone when properly applied. In fact, these principles have already been proven to work for tens of thousands of real people and influenced millions. Like them, you don't have to wait any longer to find the life you want. The only person you're waiting on is you.

HOW TO USE THE TOOLS

While this book can be read straight through from the first page to the last, your current needs may draw you to one section or another. Part one (chapters 1–4) will be the foundation of your transformation. In it, you'll learn how to chart a path toward becoming exactly who your Creator made you to be, with all the accompanying risks and rewards. But after reading part one, you may decide to skip around in part two (chapters 5–8). Read the chapters in this section in any order you like. If your mental health is of primary concern, chapter 5 might be the next logical step for you. If your physical health is currently in shambles, you may want to skip straight from part one to chapter 6. If your relationships are a mess, you might head to chapter 7. If you're underwater spiritually, chapter 8 might be the one drawing you next. Whatever order you read them in, be sure to circle back and read them all. The essence of holistic health is that we grow in all areas of our lives—body, mind, and spirit. Given your current situation, one chapter may feel more important than the others, but you need them all.

At the end of each chapter, you will see three sections: "Talk It Out," "Work It Out," and "Write It Out." These are best approached after you've read and processed each chapter in full. "Talk It Out" questions are for you to process within trusted community. While some questions must be pondered in solitude before they're addressed publicly, no one learns and grows well in isolation. We are all better together. In the "Work It Out" sections, take notes and work through key takeaways that will help you apply what you're learning to your particular life and situation. In "Write It Out," respond to the prompt as honestly as you can. This section will help you process where you are and give you space to brainstorm where to go.

As mentioned before, I wrote this book from a Judeo-Christian worldview. That means I believe in God the Father, God the Son, and God the Holy Spirit. The teachings of the Scriptures will be foundational to everything we will discuss in this book. As one connected to the ancient roots of the Christian faith and connected more to the global church than to the small American subset of Christianity, I prefer to use Hebrew names for Jesus, names like *Yeshua* and *Adonai*. I hope this won't be a distraction to anyone but instead a reminder of the faithfulness of these teachings. As we step forward together, know that we are walking an ancient path that has been trodden by generations of followers who have taken similar steps of faith across the world.

EVERY LITTLE STEP YOU TAKE

If you're feeling overwhelmed, here's some good news: You don't need to do it all right now. If a desperate situation has led you to seek change, you're already on the right track. Once you start applying what you're learning, then you're on the road to transformation—and transformation doesn't have to happen all at once.

While you don't need all the answers, all the solutions, or every little thing in place before you start making changes, it's helpful to know a few stages that you'll face on your journey:

- **Desire.** A journey toward better health has to be something you want for yourself, not something others have pressured, shamed, or forced you into. The desire starts with you.
- **Decision.** Desire alone does nothing. Your desire for transformation must lead you to exercise your agency by making a specific *decision* to change your *direction*.
- **Discomfort.** I'm going to be honest with you. Transformation, though necessary, is never easy. Even contemplating making

changes may stretch you beyond your comfort zone. If you anticipate this discomfort and prepare yourself to face it as a natural part of the process, however, it will hold less sway over you when it comes.

- **Determination.** Once you decide to change, your subconscious will immediately go to work trying to sabotage you. If your subconscious is anything like mine, it does this thing where it tries to convince you that you're going to die. You'll hear this dynamic play out in the way people who are trying to change how they eat talk about their favorite foods. "Oh," they'll say, "I couldn't live without bacon," or, "A life without butter just isn't worth living." Sometimes they're joking, but there's a serious undercurrent beneath the laughter. Your subconscious, desiring ease and comfort, wants you to believe that positive changes will actually kill you. In fact, the opposite is true. You'll need determination to override your body and brain's panicked overreactions and press forward toward transformation.

- **Drive.** Wherever you are along this scale—whether you're sensing a desire to change, making the decision to seek transformation, feeling discomfort, or seeking to press forward with determination—one thing that will keep you grounded is your motivation, your "why." Why are you doing this? What is your purpose for awakening a better you? Whenever you feel tempted to quit, reconnecting with your purpose will fill you with fresh motivation.

LEAVING THE MATRIX

Like Morpheus did with Neo, I stand in front of you now, holding out a blue pill and a red pill. If you fail to commit to your own transformation, you'll be choosing the blue pill—a seemingly safe but ultimately limiting choice that leads to a monotonous life of uninformed sameness. This may feel like a safe bet, but as Neo discovered, the blue pill will never lead to a full life.

Your other option is to choose the red pill. Leave the Matrix. Commit to your transformation, open yourself to a new reality, and see how drastically your vision of the world—and yourself—can change.

TALK IT OUT

1. Deciding to seek transformation is a key moment. What prompted your decision?
2. Seeking transformation can be a long and complicated process. What will keep you motivated along the way?

WORK IT OUT

What does it mean for you to know that you are a mess and yet deeply loved by God?

Rank from 1 to 4 the areas of your life you wish to transform, with 1 being the least important and 4 being the most important. Remember, this is a question of urgency based on your current needs. While one area might feel like a higher priority right now, becoming the person God created you to be means you will grow in each area over time.

_____ mental and emotional health
_____ physical health
_____ relational health
_____ spiritual health

WRITE IT OUT

Spend five minutes freewriting about what might be holding you back from seeking transformation.

1

High Risk, High Reward

When I first got hired as a lifeguard, I couldn't swim. It sounds unbelievable, but it's true. My first job had been as a fast-food fry cook, but my arms only had to be burned by hot grease so many times before I knew that wasn't the job I wanted. I needed a change. My mom had heard that the country club near the projects was hiring lifeguards. Apparently, the pool was having staffing issues, probably because it was in a Blood neighborhood. The fact that I could barely dog-paddle didn't even appear on Mom's radar—or mine. If it could get me out of that boiling hot kitchen, I was willing to give almost anything a shot. Even being a lifeguard.

I was up-front in the interview about my lack of swimming skills, but to my surprise, the organization hired me on the spot, saying I could learn on the job. It would be sink or swim for me—literally. I was wary, but the director promised she would work with me. She assured me I'd learn what I needed to know. I definitely almost drowned, but I stuck with the training. Perhaps more importantly, the director stuck with me. She guided my learning process and kept me on the right track, helping me apply good principles.

Under the director's guidance, I swam daily, learning the strokes and studying books on lifeguarding in my off-hours. I was putting in the work, but because I wasn't training alone or trying to handle things by myself, I advanced at a rapid rate. My body grew stronger, my swimming more secure, and my lifeguard skills became top-notch. Eventually, I was able to pass the lifeguard test and start taking shifts at the club. Life looked good from atop the lifeguard stand, and at the end of the summer, I was awarded Lifeguard of the Year.

How had I gone from grease-splattered arms to a trophy in my hands? My desperation to escape a terrible job led to taking a risk I wouldn't normally have taken—applying for a position that was above my abilities and was in the dead center of a gang neighborhood. I made a choice to seek accurate information and leverage the wisdom of an expert guide, and in doing so, I saw my prospects totally transform. Though born of desperation, my push for a new job had given me so much more than better summer employment and a trophy. It gave me a taste for agency.

CREATING AGENCY

Perhaps up till this point, you've felt that life has just been happening to you. Seasons come, seasons go, and all you do is react—never act. While there are elements to life that will always be beyond your control, there are still areas in which you can take charge and create agency today. Creating agency simply means that you take responsibility for your own life, much like Ruth did in Scripture.

Ruth didn't have a lot of choices. She was a woman from Moab who had married a son of Israel, and a recent string of deaths in the immediate family had left her in a precarious situation. Her husband, brother-in-law, and father-in-law had all died, and in that ancient patriarchal society, that meant she didn't have any means to provide for herself. Her mother-in-law, Naomi, told Ruth to return to her birth family and remarry into another household. For Ruth, that would mean remaining in Moab, going back to her clan, and returning to Moabite ways.

Instead, Ruth took her agency into her own hands. "Here's what we're going to do," she told Naomi. "We're sticking together. We're heading back to your country together. Where you're going, I'm going. Where you die, I'll die." Ruth was all in. She was a "ride or die" type of friend. Ruth could make it in the hood.

After traveling over mountains and across a desert, the women arrived back in Israel but not to a warm welcome. Naomi was a widow, which was a strike against her, and Ruth was even worse—she was both a widow and a foreigner. At every turn, they faced adversity and hardship.

Yet Ruth's agency brought her to the field of Boaz, the extended family member through whom her Creator would provide for her and her mother-in-law. By the time we hear the last of Ruth, she had gained a new husband, a home, and a child. Naomi cherished Ruth and doted on Ruth's new baby. And the women from the community declared that Ruth was better to Naomi than seven sons, an enormous compliment in those days.[1]

Ruth's transformation started when she looked at the choices in front of her and rejected them all. She exercised agency, prioritizing a relationship and family loyalty to reach something different. Through it all, Ruth's Creator blessed her. Her life ended with more joy than she had likely ever imagined possible, and the change in her trajectory began when she stepped out and began making choices.

HARNESS AGENCY

When we were little, everyone made our decisions for us, and maybe rightly so. Little kids will do anything: try to eat pinecones, ride their bikes on the roof, drink out of the toilet. But as we mature, we realize that we are capable of making informed decisions.

Harnessing your agency means you start making choices for yourself and then, after seeking complete information, you decide how best to apply what you've learned. You don't allow others to make your decisions for you, even when it's "for your own good." You control your boundaries, your involvement, and even whom you choose to take your advice from and how you apply it. In short, agency is *choice*. When you are not making a choice, that is a choice in itself. Not to decide is to decide—it's the decision to be passive and let others dictate your life.

> **Agency is *choice*.**

Your agency is not determined by your circumstances or your place in society. Like Ruth, you'll find those matters beyond your control. What you can control, however, is how you respond:

- You can see yourself as a victim or a victor.
- You can accept the status quo or push for change.
- You can view yourself as powerless or learn to exercise the power you have.

This is the essence of your agency. The choices are laid out before you, and when you take responsibility for your life in how you navigate those choices, you can move past desperation to seek the right information, apply it, and experience transformation. When you're no longer just existing—when you're fully living, wholly in control of your choices and making the best possible informed decisions—you will experience holistic health.

FOR HIS GLORY

Practicing agency doesn't mean that you rule out the work of your Creator. He created all and rules over all. But it's also important to note that when he created you, he gave you emotions, intellect, and a will. He gave you the ability to make choices. You are not a puppet or a robot. You have a mind, a heart, and a spirit. Your Creator expects you to use these responsibly—not to squander them.

One day, we will all stand before the judgment seat of our Creator and give an account of our lives. Though overflowing with love and compassion, our Creator is also all-seeing, all-knowing, wise, and perfectly just. He will not hold us responsible for matters that were beyond our control. But he also knows exactly which matters those were. Your Creator knows what choices you could have made and the areas where you simply shrugged and moved on without even trying. When you give your account, will you be able to say you made the very most of the one precious life he's given you?

SEEING YOUR OPTIONS

You really can chart a new path. By making choices about what you want to accept and what you want to reject from what life has handed you, you can strike out and claim something different for yourself. But here's the kicker: I can't tell you exactly what your steps will look like because those steps depend on you and your ultimate destination.

Nobody's path is the same; therefore, nobody's journeys will look identical. For me, I wanted to be a lifeguard, so that meant learning to swim. For you, the steps will look totally different because your destination is different. When it comes to transformation, there's no packaged system or one-size-fits-all plan.

You can create your own agency. You can awaken a better you.

I can't tell you exactly what your next move is. It's through exercising your own agency that the next step will reveal itself to you. What I can do is shine a light ahead and show you that the path you're currently walking can diverge—and you can choose which direction you want to take. You can create your own agency. You can awaken a better you.

TALK IT OUT

1. What does it mean to exercise agency over your own life?
2. Describe a time when you exercised agency. What did that situation look like? What were the results?
3. How will exercising your agency change your life?

WORK IT OUT

List three areas of your life in which you're currently exerting your agency:

Look back on page 13 at the transformation areas you ranked. In your top two areas, pinpoint at least three specific things you want to gain control over in the coming days. If you were to practice agency in those areas, what might that look like? What could potentially change?

WRITE IT OUT

Spend five minutes freewriting about agency. Brainstorm steps you might take toward leveraging your power to choose for your own good and for the good of others.

2

The Value of You

When I was a junior in high school, I got into a verbal altercation with a young lady. Things escalated, and she said to me, "Imma let my brothers know. They see you, they're gonna beat you." She was referring not to biological brothers but to her three best friends, who were all males. We'd grown up together, so there was no need for her to name them. I knew exactly who she was talking about. I needed to stay ready. One of these brothers lived right down the street, and the others were always around. As soon as they saw me, it would be on.

I didn't have to wait long. One brother was proactive and called me on the phone, telling me to meet him at the park. I pulled on my boots and my fighting clothes, making sure my jeans were snug and my belt cinched tight. I strutted down to that park, ready. I was meeting a brother for hand-to-hand combat, and I would prove myself. Everyone watching would be in awe. When I arrived, however, nobody was there to witness what went down. No crowd, no homies—not even the girl who had started it all.

Eventually, I would be happy there were no witnesses. At the moment, though, I had to adjust my expectations. I tugged my belt tighter and rolled my head around on my neck. As long as I was here and he was here, we had all we needed.

We went at it.

I quickly felt myself getting the advantage and knew I would win the fight. That's when I decided to have some fun. I'd grown up watching WWE and had always wanted to try out one of the Hardy Boyz's signature finishing moves. No ladders or folding chairs required for this one, which was perfect, given the setting. It was time to finish this dude. I reached around and grabbed him in a headlock. I held him in a tight clutch, bent forward at the waist. I knew exactly what to do next.

Clutching my opponent's neck tight, I would run forward, jump in the air, and brace myself for our glorious, final crash to the ground. After which I would bounce to my feet, victorious and taunting, while he rolled around in the dust clutching his back. This is exactly what happens when the Hardy Boyz do this move, and I couldn't wait to experience it in real time. This was game over, lights out. Groans, crying, and hands over the face.

But when I tried it, that's not what happened. I jumped in the air, bracing for impact—but my guy barely moved. He turned his head, gazing up at me in utter bafflement, eyebrows drawn together. "Dude . . . what are you doing?"

If not for the fact that I had so clearly beaten him already, my humiliation would have been complete. This story still gets me every time.

Now, remember, this dude is just one of three. Fresh from my victory in the park (embarrassing, but still a win), I decided not to run from the other two fights that were certainly awaiting me any day now. After school, I could have taken the city bus home to delay the inevitable, but I chose instead to jump on the school bus. No use avoiding it.

As the bus was pulling to my stop, I looked up and saw a little crowd gathered. I'd been dozing off, but I jolted awake at the sound of the second dude shouting curses, demanding that I get off the bus. That explained the crowd. They'd been waiting for me.

I'd just had a long day at school and I was tired, but here I was walking into a herd of kids, really about to do this. I stepped off the bus, the classic chant "Fight! Fight! Fight!" echoing in my ears.

The difference between the first dude and this second one was that this one was five to six inches taller, sixty to seventy pounds heavier, and much stronger. This was more of a David and Goliath situation, and now I didn't even have the hope of a secret wrestling move to fall back on. We both knew I was in trouble. As we walked down the street a ways, preparing for hand-to-hand combat, the look in his eyes was unmistakable: "You're done."

The moment we were a safe distance from the bus stop, he lunged toward me, leveraging his reach and throwing huge hay-makers. But here's what he didn't know: Though my wrestling wasn't on point, my boxing was. I'd been practicing. I bobbed and weaved, leaning forward and arching back. I was Neo on the roof-top. He missed fifteen to twenty punches in a row.

I waited for my moment, wound back, closed my eyes, and threw all my weight behind a sizzling right jab.

Pow.

I landed that one punch, and he flew back ten feet.

There he sat, cartoon birds flying in circles over his head—half because I'd rung his bell and half in disbelief over what had just happened. But he wasn't the only one shocked. I couldn't believe it either. It's a good thing that the first punch landed, though, because in throwing it, I'd dislocated my shoulder. I couldn't have done anything else if I wanted to. But before he got up, just in case, I pushed against my shoulder to pop it back in.

Turns out it didn't matter. The punch was so hard and the aftermath so embarrassing that this dude just quit. The fight was over. The whole crowd knew it, including that third brother I was supposed to fight. When he saw me take out this behemoth with one blow and casually pop my own shoulder back into its socket, he wanted no part of me.

That is what can happen in life. When you show people you're unstoppable—when you refuse to surrender to losses, when you keep your head up and fight for yourself, when you step into the next challenge and smash it straight on the jaw—you start collecting wins. When people see you're taking on big challenges and no longer running, they take notice. They get with you or they get out of the way.

Yes, I could have gotten myself whupped. It could have been bad. And sure, I've taken some L's. But not that day.

That day? I knocked out a giant, not because I was stronger than he was but because I'd been intent on my training and learned to use what I had. I had a great weaving game—some real Floyd Mayweather action—and that, combined with one punch, was all I needed.

When you stop being afraid to step out and use what you have, you will clear the obstacles in front of you and prevail. When you see that what you have is all you need. When you name your strengths, recognize them, and see that they have value—and so do you. Access to that information—knowing the strengths, value, and essence of you—puts you one step further down the road to transformation.

> **When you stop being afraid to step out and use what you have, you will clear the obstacles in front of you and prevail.**

KNOWING WHO YOU ARE

Knowing who you are starts with telling your story. That doesn't mean glossing over the awkward and uncomfortable parts. That means peeling back the facade and being honest about the depths of who you are and what you've experienced—hood childhood, sixth-grade graduation meltdown, embarrassing wrestling moves, and all.

If we were sitting over cups of coffee right now and I asked you to tell me about yourself, where would you start? How would you explain yourself to me? I'm not asking if you could tell me facts about yourself, like your marital status, what you do for a living, and whether you watch *Game of Thrones*. I'm asking if you could honestly explain who you are and why you are that way. Could you step back and look at your history in all its complexities and understand the forces that have shaped you and how they have created the very real value that only you bring to the table?

If that prospect sounds daunting, it could be because so many of us have never had to describe in detail who we are outside a job interview (when you have to explain your worst quality is overworking, smh). Perhaps you've never truly contemplated what it means to understand your own story. Knowing your story is a sober and valuable thing, and before you can explain yourself to anyone else, you must first explain yourself to you.

> **The degree to which you can explain yourself to you is the degree to which you will awaken a better you.**

Let me repeat that just in case you missed it. Before you can explain yourself to anyone else, you must first master the art and science of explaining *yourself* to *you*. The degree to which you can explain yourself to you is the degree to which you will awaken a better you. It's more than an interview skill, though. Knowing yourself intimately starts with intentional introspection.

EXPLAINING YOU TO YOU: A FIVE-STEP GUIDE

To take hold of your agency and ensure you're in the driver's seat of your own life, you'll first need to understand who you really are. Here are five steps you can take to start explaining you to yourself.

Step One: Assess Nature

Your nature is a set of unavoidable attributes inherited through your DNA that would be present no matter where you were born in the world, when you lived, and who raised you.

Inherited traits include a variety of characteristics:

- your hair color/texture, eye color, and skin color
- which hand you write with
- whether you suffer from allergies
- how tall you will grow
- what genetic diseases/disorders you may be susceptible to

Whether you know your family of origin well or not, there's a definite genetic component to your natural development.

While we may joke about not wanting to become our parents, our genetic predispositions often make some things inevitable. In studies involving biological twins raised apart, behavioral geneticists have discovered that genetic predispositions could play a role in shaping behavior. Twins raised apart in very different home environments often develop in strikingly similar ways, including their habits, choices, and interests.[1]

Depending on your experience with your family of origin—including whether you know anything about your genetic lineage at all—this point may strike you differently. I recognize that. I also recognize that if we're seeking to understand ourselves, it would be foolish to overlook this point. In the most basic sense, you are deeply affected by your genetics, which means that regardless of race, gender, or education, certain core factors will still be true.

Once you have a handle on the story of your nature, you don't need to rely on outside voices to tell you who you are. You're in a much better position to step into the world on your own terms. You'll also be in a better position to understand how the distinct ways in which you were nurtured may have influenced who you've become.

STEP TWO: EVALUATE NURTURE

Beyond the natural factors discussed previously, we're also impacted by the surroundings in which we were raised—both what they looked like and how we responded to them.

Family of Origin

Healthy, challenging, good, or bad—your family of origin is the most significant factor in how you were nurtured. Because we are most vulnerable and impressionable as babies and children, our families inform how we see ourselves and experience the world.

My family life played a major role in my development. My parents both left school early, and my mother was a teenager when I was born. Whether I like it or not, these were major factors influencing my development—as were the facts that I was well-loved and provided for, that I was the firstborn, and that I was raised in a Black American home. A change in any one of those details could have altered the trajectory of my life.

To consider how your family of origin has influenced your natural development, you must start by analyzing three specific elements:

- **Ethnic heritage.** The ethnic heritage of your family can impact everything from the languages you speak to the foods you eat, games you enjoy, cultural streams you navigate, jokes you understand, and traits you value in others. Ethnic heritage can determine which religions you understand (or fear), the unspoken philosophies that shape your thoughts and guide your decisions, and your comfort levels with personal touch. While the list could go on, the basic truth is this: Ethnic heritage deeply shapes us.

    My family's ethnic culture is Black American. That means being part of a collective community rather than being merely an individual—seeing life through the lens of the Black community.
- **Family culture.** Family cultures develop *within* their cultures of origin and vary from household to household. On some level, the behavior that is normalized within your family can set your internal expectations for the rest of your life.

    For me, growing up in a Black American family meant memorizing every line in *The Color Purple*. Knowing that once I went outside, the only way to get water was from the water hose because I "smelled like outside" now. It meant waking up to the sound of Anita Baker and being engulfed in the scent of Pine-Sol whenever it was time to clean the house.
- **Birth order.** Scientific studies have demonstrated interesting links between birth order and personality traits: firstborns tend to be leaders, middle children inventive, and lastborns charming. If you're an only child, you likely carry the traits of firstborns, just on more intense levels.[2] There are exceptions and caveats to all these assertions, of course, but understanding how birth order affects

development can help you understand yourself and your partici-
pation in group dynamics.

For me, being the oldest meant having a heightened sense of
carefulness, given that there was nobody my age to model behavior. It meant being responsible for the poor behavior of my siblings when we were all together. In the words of my mother when
I'd ask why I was the one in trouble, "Because you're the oldest.
They're younger and immature, but you know better." To this day,
I'm still processing this with my counselor.

Community Conditioning

Beyond your family of origin, the community in which you were
raised played a major role in shaping who you have become. This
is about more than just geography. Your community is the backdrop of your life. Did you grow up in an urban, rural, or suburban
area? Upper, middle, or lower class? Blue collar or white collar?
What were the resources and realities of your neighborhood? Was
the population density high or low? Was your environment vio-
lent? Privileged? Competitive? Casual? Did you experience gang
violence? How was your high school experience? Such matters
have a long-term impact on your psyche.

We will discuss unresolved trauma in more detail soon, but for
now, know that the specific social pressures you experienced in
your community had lasting effects, even if they currently go unrecognized. If you don't understand how your background has
shaped you, you will understand neither yourself nor how you relate to others.

According to the Pew Research Center, both urban and rural
residents in the United States "feel misunderstood and looked
down on by Americans living in other types of communities.
About two-thirds or more in urban and rural areas say people in
other types of communities don't understand the problems people

face in their communities. And majorities of urban and rural residents say people who don't live in their type of community have a negative view of those who do."[3] Because they feel hurt, misunderstood, and unheard, both groups operate out of fear, making them easy targets for political manipulation. Recognizing this pattern is a good first step toward investigating how your community's culture has formed you, how it can be used against you, and how it can be leveraged for success.

STEP THREE: PONDER PERSONAL CHOICES

Although many of the factors listed previously were beyond your control, they're not the only factors that have shaped who you've become. No matter where, when, or into what family you were born, you still have a say in what sort of person you become. Perhaps you made different choices than your parents did. You moved across the country. You joined the army. Chose a faith that wasn't your family's religion. Invested in higher education. Broke a family cycle. Maybe, like my mom, you had a baby at seventeen. All these decisions are key points in your story. Knowing what they are and how they impacted your trajectory helps you explain you to you.

Shortly after I left home, I realized that I had never quite learned how to be an adult. Nothing I'd learned at home seemed to transfer into adult life. That's when it hit me. I'd been raised by a teenage mom. How could she teach me how to do all the adult things when she was still learning how to be an adult herself? This realization impacted me deeply. I could have left it at that. I could have just learned something about myself and moved on. But I wasn't about to let this gem fall by the wayside. Instead, I chose to specifically incorporate skill development into my coaching plans. When I understood how my personal history shaped me, I chose to act on that knowledge, which made me a more empathetic coach. My growth hasn't just benefited me—it's made all the difference for my clients as well.

> **SHAPED BY THE SPIRIT**
>
> If you are a follower of Yeshua, remember that you're also continuously being shaped by the Spirit of God. In Scripture, we're reminded that we don't have to be formed by the world—we can be transformed through the renewing of our minds.[4]

STEP FOUR: PINPOINT YOUR PERSONALITY

Personality tests are popular, and for good reason. They provide both a frame of reference and terms we can use to relate to others. But even the best test is still generic. While a test may show where you fall on a spectrum, it can't account for *why* you have developed the traits you have. Are they inherent to your nature or adaptive mechanisms you developed to cope with your environment? To answer these questions, you must dig deeper.

I've found this greatly helpful in my own life. I used to think there was something wrong with me because I couldn't really enjoy the big moments—the wins, the successes, the peak experiences. While others seemed to glory in such moments, I did not. Having not grown up in an environment that discussed personality typing in any way, I was well into adulthood before I realized I was actually an introvert. That might not sound like a big deal to you, but imagine being in your mid-thirties thinking you're an extrovert and then finding out the entire time you were an introvert acting like a grumpy extrovert.

I've since learned that introverts—particularly introverted leaders—possess a trait termed *carefulness*. Basically, that means introverts carry a heightened awareness of risk. While carefulness can make me a better leader in one sense (I'm less likely to go off the rails and take all of Build a Better Us down with me), it can also rob me of my joy in leveling up.[5] This dynamic explains why I've often failed to feel joy and fully experience big moments. The more I get to know this aspect of my personality, the less I worry that there's something wrong with me. Instead, I accept my reactions as a part of my unique nature, set aside my concerns, and press forward. Knowing myself better has literally helped me awaken a better me.

Step Five: Grow Your Giftedness

From a spiritual standpoint, everyone in the service of Yeshua has been granted spiritual gifts.[6] From a natural standpoint, God's also granted everyone intrinsic skills and abilities. You may have a gift with words, possessing the seemingly effortless ability to edify, encourage, or speak truth to power. You might possess extreme physical coordination, allowing you to break-dance, backflip, or juke. You may be musical, analytical, artistic, or highly relational. Recognizing your giftedness is a major aspect of understanding yourself.

Unfortunately, many of us sail through life unaware of our giftedness, sometimes because what we do comes so naturally to us that we don't recognize our gifts as extraordinary. In most cases, people move through life on autopilot, operating unconsciously without fostering their gifts. As a result, many gifts go underdeveloped and underused. To prevent this from happening, you must recognize the necessity of not just identifying your natural gifts but also nurturing them.

I wasn't always aware I had the ability to help others gain agency over their lives. I gave people advice, sure—but we all do that. After a while though, I noticed a pattern. I would talk with someone, then they would tell me, "I feel inspired. I never saw myself like that." It was through a multitude of advisers and conversations, not just one person, that I came to recognize a consistent theme throughout the scope of my story: No matter where I was or what I was doing, I was always helping people, and that process of helping came more easily to me than it did to others.

I know my gift and it comes naturally, but that doesn't mean I don't need to hone my skills. On the contrary, I work on them. I coach people, read, talk with key friends, and have long conversations with healthy people from different perspectives. Along the way, I work out new ideas within the context of my community. I'm around colleagues with high discernment. Friends with high emotional intelligence. Mentors and mentees who allow for push and pull as we speak into each other's lives.

I nurture my gifts every single day so I can be the best version of myself possible—and you need to do the same. Only once you identify and cultivate your God-given gifts can you begin to exercise them intentionally, not just intuitively. That's what makes any gift a truly useful tool.

When it comes to knowing and understanding yourself, you must carefully account for and fully consider every aspect of your story: nature, nurture, choices, personality, and giftedness. Once you have a solid understanding of the foundation of you—always starting with the realization that you are deeply loved by God— then you can weather any storm that comes your way. There will always be people who try to disrupt and contort your understanding of who you are. But when you know yourself, you're able to recognize your own worth—something no one else can take away.

TALK IT OUT

1. How will seeking to know ourselves give us more accurate information with which to engage the world?
2. Which of the steps to knowing yourself do you feel you've overlooked up to this point? How could giving attention to that area change your life?

WORK IT OUT

List at least three specific strengths inherent to your nature:

How might these strengths be leveraged to your advantage?

List at least three specific weaknesses inherent to your nature:

How might these weaknesses be appropriately addressed?

List specific tendencies you've developed as the result of the following factors:

Family of Origin

Community Conditioning

Personal Choices

WRITE IT OUT

Spend five minutes freewriting about the importance of knowing yourself. Brainstorm steps by which you can come to a better understanding of who you are and what's shaped you.

3

On the Red Carpet

I once found myself standing on a red carpet. The whole thing was surreal. I was accompanying a friend who actually belonged there, but about two steps in, it felt pretty clear that I did not.

It was a whole scene. Cameras flashing, people bumping past, eyes darting, microphones ready. The crowd naturally gravitated toward certain individuals for information, autographs, and interviews. By watching the flow, I could see which artists and entertainers currently ranked highest on the industry's value meter. For those happy few, the red carpet seemingly validated their worth.

Then there was me. It was hard to know how to feel. I was bopping along with my friend, bumping into people of influence who had impacted me from afar, but I wasn't enjoying the experience as much as I'd anticipated. More than anything else, I felt invisible. For all the attention anyone paid to me, I may as well have been a lamppost—out of place, incongruent, and totally unnecessary.

I'm typically pretty confident about who I am and the value I bring regardless of the environment, but in that moment, I started questioning my entire life. Had I really accomplished anything?

Had I wasted my life pursuing those degrees and credentials? Should I drop everything and learn to produce beats so I could drop a fire track that would have everybody singing my song? I was that GIF of Raven-Symoné chewing gum in real time.

That's what red-carpet moments do. They force us to examine ourselves in seriously uncomfortable ways. A red carpet is nothing more than a conveyor belt of value. As someone who was there for no other reason than to support a friend, I shouldn't have taken it all so personally. Yet I couldn't stop wondering: Is what I do even important? Am *I* important?

RED-CARPET MOMENTS

Like it or not, at some point, we will all have red-carpet moments and be forced to consider how others see and experience us in the world. These moments lay our personhood bare, demanding that we prove ourselves. It's shocking how quickly it can happen. One minute you're minding your own business; the next, you're suddenly questioning your entire existence and feeling terrible about yourself.

These days, you don't need to have a friend who happens to be decently known or famous to face your own red carpet. Social media has made red-carpet moments more frequent and universal. The internet has sneakily given rise to

> Red-carpet moments lay our personhood bare, demanding that we prove ourselves.

a nearly unavoidable red-carpet existence, affecting all of us every time we log on.

Every day from the comfort of our couches or, if we're honest, our bathrooms, we're dropped directly onto a digital red carpet. Instead of seeing ourselves in the context of our immediate environment, we're now seeking to find a place in the grand scheme of global society.

When I was growing up, people always said, "Don't try to keep up with the Joneses," meaning don't get caught up comparing everything you do to the people around you. Forget keeping up with the Joneses. Now we gotta keep up with the Kardashians. The effects of this on the psyche can be devastating. Most of us can't dance like Diddy. Aren't funny like Chappelle or Ellen. Not cool like Childish Gambino or smart like Elon Musk. Not counting those heated debates over whether a dress is white and gold or blue and black—for the record, it was gold—most of us are living basic lives and fronting online. From the looks of our timelines, we'll never become internet influencers. Some of our pictures get fewer than ten likes, one of which came from Mom.

Love it or hate it, this model for social interaction doesn't seem to be going away, and it comes with some serious downsides. Studies have already proven the more social media sites someone uses, the higher their rates of depression and anxiety.[1] Young women who browse social media sites of attractive peers experience worsening body image issues.[2] The more time people spend online, the lonelier they feel.[3]

While your experience may vary based on personality type and individual response, there's solid evidence that this social dynamic is affecting us. In order to keep our Instagram poppin', we must produce a nonstop stream of content: activities, events, pictures, hot takes, and fresh experiences. In effect, this leads us to a performance-based life in which we try to live up to other people's estimations of who we are rather than rooting our transformation deeply in who we already know ourselves to be.

Comparing ourselves to others—to people with different family backgrounds, community contexts, personality types, ethnic heritages, and giftedness—will only strip us of our confidence and disrupt our transformation. We must always be on guard for such red-carpet moments because they're not limited to our phones.

RED-CARPET ENVIRONMENTS

Certain environments seem to foster more red-carpet responses than others. For some people, it's the gym. Everyone lined up in front of all those mirrors, side by side as if begging for comparison. You try to keep your eyes straight ahead, but they wander. You notice who has a flat stomach, rippling abs, thunder thighs. You spot who has to yank their workout pants up over a roll of belly fat and who's using the lightest set of weights. Who's pressing a crazy amount? Who's killing it on the rower? You silently keep track, turning it all into an unspoken competition while hoping no one peeks at your numbers.

Maybe the gym isn't a problem for you. Maybe it's the classroom. The office. The recording studio. A mommy-and-me playgroup. Your annual family reunion. Someone always has higher grades, more accounts, bigger hits, better lives. Wherever the place may be, you'll recognize it as a red-carpet environment because it makes you feel that you need to prove yourself by outperforming others.

RESPONDING TO RED CARPETS

Though red carpets can appear anywhere, that doesn't mean we're powerless to face them. Just by knowing how to recognize them, we rob them of a great measure of their power. Beyond that, we can come to understand our own reactions to these moments and learn how best to counter that gut reaction. For the most part, red carpets trigger two specific responses: We either perform for the occasion or deflate in despair.

Those Who Perform

Those who perform for the occasion aren't just the people who have figured out how to work the system to their advantage. At their core, these people are naturally performance driven. This type will scope out the situation, assess how it works, and formulate a plan for achievement. But the more you successfully perform without introspection, the more easily you lose touch with who you are. One day you realize your life has morphed into a never-ending performance tailored for whomever you're currently seeking to please.

If you recognize this tendency in yourself, beware. The more you adjust your behavior to match an external expectation, the more you're actually being controlled by the need for people's approval. Instead of you working the system, the system is working you.

Those Who Deflate

While some people can perform, others just deflate. Judging themselves incapable of meeting the gold standard, they pull in like a turtle retreating into its shell, avoiding the sort of effort that would invite scrutiny.

If you recognize yourself in this description, beware the cost of pulling back out of self-preservation. When you give up on your passions simply because you believe you can't reach the levels others achieve, you sabotage your own potential and end up robbing the world of the beauty living inside of you.

The Key

Whether red-carpet moments cause you to perform or deflate, the key to putting your response in check is to focus less on others and more on yourself. Rather than comparing your height, weight, and reach to the giant waiting for you at the bus stop, lean into your particular strengths and hone them.

When you consider that there are nearly eight billion people on the planet, this whole comparison game stands in a different light.[4] Remembering that you are one of billions brings a sobriety that keeps you humble, and it keeps you serious about not comparing yourself to others. You are unique to this world. You are exceptional, with a God-given purpose that only you can fulfill. The wild combination of elements such as your background, your upbringing, your experiences, and your talents (developed both through nature and nurture) make you one of a kind. The way to overcome red-carpet moments is to double down on who you are and invest in intentionally nurturing those aspects that make you unique.

In 2013, Kobe Bryant revealed in an interview that part of his practice routine at the time involved not leaving the court after practice until he'd made four hundred shots. When asked how he'd know when he'd made four hundred, he seemed incredulous. "What do you mean, How do I know? . . . I know because I counted them."[5]

You won't reap where you haven't sown.[6] Sow intentionally, and you will reap the benefits in your own life. Invest in and cultivate your unique gifts and skills, and you'll be able to stand on the

> **You won't reap where you haven't sown.**

red carpet next to your famous friends without wondering if you should risk it all and drop a rap album—whether you have demonstrated musical or lyrical gifts or not. That isn't to say you'll never feel the lure of the red carpet. These moments happen naturally in the ebb and flow of life. You will experience pressure and feel off balance. When you sense that happening, remember that navigating red-carpet moments doesn't require IQ so much as it does EQ (emotional intelligence):

1. **Take time to be emotionally introspective.** Get in touch with what you're feeling. Ask yourself what's prompting these emotions. Are they rational or irrational responses? Investigate and fully process your feelings.

2. **Connect to community.** Reach out to trusted people—peers and mentors, especially. Process what you're thinking and feeling, and let voices that have proven themselves trustworthy over time speak into your life.

3. **Compose a list of sober truths.** Write down things you know to be true outside the press of your current emotions. List your gifts, skills, and current goals. Remind yourself of everything you've been learning about you who are and who your Creator made you to be.

4. **Start gradually applying what you have discovered about yourself.** One of the best antidotes to worrying about whether you're enough is to be fully and honestly present in your own life. Identify your gifts. Nurture your skills. Put what you're learning into practice. Awaken a better you.

WAKING UP TO YOU

Learning your own value isn't about fitting in on a red carpet. It's about understanding yourself. Loving yourself. Growing in your ability to leverage your unique assets. When you're able to do this effectively, you can see that there's no shame in being different. In fact, what makes you different is often your superpower!

The process isn't easy. It takes time, attention, and a concerted effort. But it's worth it. When you know yourself and consider that your life has a unique purpose, you learn to distinguish what will work for you and what won't. Instead of defaulting to what we've seen work in the lives of people we admire, we need to exercise courage and risk trying new things. There's no way to know for sure until you try. You may be scared, and that's understandable. But don't let fear hold you back forever. Some choices require us to make the leap while we're still afraid—and that's okay. You can still take that first, faltering step. You can live fully and express yourself joyfully in the world. You *can* awaken a better you.

TALK IT OUT

1. Describe a memorable red-carpet moment. How did it make you feel? What was your reaction? How might you respond differently in the future?
2. How has social media affected your life and your friendships? What are the positive and negative aspects of social media?

WORK IT OUT

In the moment, red carpets can make us feel powerless. But we can rob them of their control with a little pre-planning and the right mindset. Use the following space to proactively prepare for future red-carpet moments, including actions you can take to handle them.

Connect to community: Make a list of people you can turn to when faced with red-carpet moments. People who know you well and will remind you of who you are.

Compose a list of sober truths: Write down your skills, gifts, and current goals. Remind yourself of what you've learned about who the Creator made you to be.

Nurture who you are: From your list of sober truths, write three things you can do to intentionally nurture who you are and work toward your goals.

WRITE IT OUT

Spend five minutes freewriting about facing red carpets. What type of red-carpet moments do you typically face, and how will your approach to them change moving forward?

4

Beware the Wiz

When I was in my twenties, I found myself doing the last thing in the world I expected. I was in the back of a truck, stacking boxes for delivery. This was my job. My life. All day long, I lifted, sorted, and hauled other people's orders, scanning tags and checking shipping labels.

There's nothing wrong with this type of work. If it's your calling, keep at it. It just wasn't how I wanted to spend my time—nor was this what God had created me to do. I felt no sense of joy or fulfillment in my work, and in no way did hauling boxes help me walk in my purpose. As a result, I battled feelings of insignificance every day.

I was a cog in the machine—unsung, unrecognized, and unknown. Another Black man working for minimum wage while seemingly less talented people moved upward and onward with their lives. This couldn't be my life. I knew I was made for more than this. But I was stuck. The longer I stayed stuck, the more I began to question my own value and worth, feeling trapped in more ways than one, boxed in both by society's labels and my own inability to exercise agency. How had I gotten here?

NOT IN HARLEM ANYMORE

When I was growing up in the eighties, there was *The Wizard of Oz* and there was *The Wiz*. If you've never seen it, just know that *The Wiz* is the Black soul version of *The Wizard of Oz* with Diana Ross as Dorothy coming from the projects and Michael Jackson as the Scarecrow. Nothing was better for the hood. *The Wiz* may not have become a mainstream success, but it's a Black classic. As a matter of fact, a failure to know at least the plot and characters of this movie could get your proverbial Black card revoked.

In the film, Dorothy is blown by a snowstorm into the strange Land of Oz. In this new world, Dorothy experiences complete and total displacement. The world she knew is gone, and she finds herself adjusting to totally new customs and patterns, just like I did when my family moved from the hood to the burbs. Then Lena Horne magicks a pair of silver shoes onto Dorothy's feet, telling her she'll never make it home to Harlem without first visiting the Wiz.

Dorothy gathers a crew and heads toward Emerald City, and each member of the squad endures much trial and tribulation, facing scary obstacles in their quest for value. A brain, a heart, courage—they are each looking for something, convinced they'll never flourish without it, convinced they need a wizard to magic it into their lives.

When they arrive at the journey's end, however, they discover the truth. The Wiz, the guy handing out everyone's value, is just a man—none other than Richard Pryor—hiding behind a curtain with a rope. The things they thought they needed the Wiz to help them with, they already had the ability to accomplish themselves.[1]

So many systems, structures, and societal messages in our world will give you the wrong information, particularly about who holds the power. They'll tell you that left on your own, you're incapable of change and growth. That you have no agency and no options. That by yourself, you're nothing. That you need the help of the Wiz to succeed. These messages are so prevalent that we often aren't even aware we've swallowed them until we find ourselves in the back of a truck, slinging boxes and wondering if this is all there is.

Though you may feel trapped, powerless, and stuck under the weight of a wizard, you can exert your own agency to poke holes in the hermetic seal, creating porous boundaries through which fresh air and new life flow. It all starts with recognizing wizards and calling them out for what they are.

MEET THE WIZARDS

A wizard desires you in a role, not a relationship. Relationships come with a sense of mutuality as you both offer and receive advice and counsel. You may be guided by the advice of someone you're in a relationship with, but you always have a voice and can make your own decisions. A role, however, is less relational and more transactional. In a role, you feel like you can't possibly succeed apart from the approval or blessing of the wizard or like you can't possibly achieve without going to that one person and that one person alone for guidance. If this describes your situation, then you've been caught by a wizard.

Almost anyone in your life can take on a wizard-like role if you grant them the authority that only God and the Scriptures should have. Though they're often people in places of special importance or authority in our lives, such as bosses, spouses, parents, or mentors, they can also be friends, siblings, neighbors, or our communities.

Often, we are caught in their web before we realize it. Perhaps a desperate situation leads us to seek information about how to break free of whatever is holding us back, so we look for advice. Without knowing it, we've set ourselves up to fall prey to a wizard.

Here's where I want to be very clear. It's important to find a guide to help you navigate the right information and seek proper application. Scripture reminds us that there's safety in a multitude of counselors.[2] But whomever we seek for counsel must first demonstrate their competence through proof of concept. Someone with a string of failed businesses shouldn't be your main source for business advice, and your cousin with the rocky marriage hasn't exactly earned the right to speak into your relationships.

It's vital that you don't allow the place of a guide to be filled by a wizard. In seeking information, problems arise when (1) you take advice from someone offering no proof of concept or (2) when you allow one—and only one—person's estimation of you to become the touchstone of your whole life.

Though many people will seek to give you advice and guide your journey, not everyone has the right to do so. No one has walked in your shoes but you. Others may see part of who you are, but nobody sees everything except you and your Creator. Though perhaps well intentioned, the wizards of this world base their advice on limited knowledge. As a result, a wizard's advice will line up more with what they *see* you to be rather than what you were *created* to be. When we allow wizards to dictate our estimation of our worth and value, our vision for ourselves shrinks—and with it, our grasp on our agency.

WIZARDS BEHIND THE CURTAIN

Unfortunately, wizards don't arise only from the physical realm. Your enemy, Satan, also uses wizards to create the illusion that your value finds its source in something other than your Creator.

Though what Satan says may make sense in the short term, in the long run, his evaluation of your worth is always a cheap substitute.

Think of how Satan manipulated Adam and Eve. He told them, "You can be like God," which sounds enticing until you realize they already were like God. They were literally made in his image. They just hadn't realized the full implications of what that meant. Satan became a wizard to Adam and Eve when he convinced them that they needed him in order to achieve something that God had already accomplished. In other words, he was giving them the wrong information about themselves and their place in the world.

It's worth noting that Satan offered Adam and Eve something he could never give them because he never possessed it in the first place. Only humankind is made in the image of God—Satan and the other heavenly beings can make no such claim.

Satan's playbook hasn't altered since then. He is hell-bent on discouraging us from seeing who we really are and what God created us to be, stringing us along with promises of cheap, flashy substitutes.

Why does he bother? What does he hope to gain?

Something similar happens when Dorothy first meets the Wiz. Their first conversation goes something like this:

DOROTHY: Can you help us, sir?

WIZ: What's in it for me?

DOROTHY: We'd be very grateful.

WIZ: (*laughing*) How 'bout your pretty slippers?[3]

By demanding that Dorothy give up her seemingly insignificant slippers in exchange for a ticket home, the Wiz is asking her for the very thing that will ultimately help her fulfill her purpose to get home. Dorothy didn't need an exchange. She needed the correct information about what she already had.

When acting the part of a wizard, Satan operates in a similar manner. If he can keep you from knowing the truth and seeing the value in who God has already created you to be, he can keep you from realizing your potential, exercising your agency, and proving yourself dangerous to his counterfeit kingdom.

LIES THAT GRANT THE WIZARDS POWER

Our world bleeds lies. Satan's explicit lies. Society's implicit ones. Our friends lie, our neighbors lie, our family and loved ones lie, and let's be honest—we also lie. Unfortunately, there are three specific lies that feed our tendency to turn to wizards.

LIE 1: "YOU ARE JUST A _____."

Perhaps the most subtle of all the wizards in your life are the lies you believe—both the ones you're told and the ones you tell yourself. As a complex individual, you're informed by multifaceted thoughts, ideas, backgrounds, and emotions. However, because complexity makes people uncomfortable, they often seek a quick fix—a shortcut to understanding you. The solution is often oversimplification. Boiling you down to bullet points. Flattening your story into something tame and ordinary.

The problems with this approach are many, but this is the bottom line: People think they can look at you, tick their mental boxes, and move on without ever really knowing you. This is especially true for those of us who don't fit well into society's prepared molds.

The desire for oversimplification drives people to use labels—particularly labels they think of as negative. Liberal. Conspiracy theorist. Social Marxist. Anti-vaxxer. Critical race theorist. Radical feminist. Beta male. Racist. Troublemaker. Victim. Even if you reject the tenets of these ideals, to save themselves time and energy, some people will do whatever mental gymnastics necessary to allow them to dismiss you, feel safe, and move on. It's easier for them to hammer you into a pre-formed social construct than to hear your story and recognize the unique strengths your experiences have instilled in you.

The labels land like hammer blows, and it isn't easy to stand against them. Our once-strong understanding of who we are ends in lies: "I'm worthless. I'm not attractive. I'm just a_____."

In *The Wiz*, Dorothy's entire quest was based on a lie—that she was just a lost girl in need of a wizard in order to make it home to Harlem. Had Dorothy recognized the lie woven to diminish her value, she could have been back home in a heartbeat, skipping all the drama and messiness in Oz. In the end, she already had everything she needed. So did the Cowardly Lion, the Tin Man, and the Scarecrow. The things they thought they needed, they already had. Like them, you, too, have everything you need.

When you take the time to know yourself and you have accurate information—when you see yourself as your Creator sees you—then everything changes. You may think you're *just* a woman, *just* a minority, *just* a single parent, *just* an immigrant, *just* a high school dropout, or *just* another Black man in America. If that's what you think, then it could be you'll never be more than that. But the word *just* is a lie. You're not "just" anything.

> When you trust God to dictate your worth and value, your vision for yourself grows—and with it, your agency.

God made you and named you who you are for a reason; your name is not derived from how others label you but from who you are purposed to be. Do not let society name you. Ask Adonai: "What is my name that supersedes how people see me and expect me to function?" When you trust God to dictate your worth and value, your vision for yourself grows—and with it, your agency.

LIE 2: YOUR IDENTITY IS DERIVED FROM WHAT YOU ACCOMPLISH.

Some people think of God primarily as a God of instructions. Though Scripture does include laws and principles, it reveals so much more about who our Creator is and how he moves. God isn't concerned with just instructions but also with information and interconnection. God doesn't just tell you what to do. He also tells you who you are. That's exciting. It's also scary.

For many of us, being truly seen and truly known is terrifying. Ironically, that's why wizards have an inherent appeal. Though they're demanding, they give us some sort of bar by which we can estimate our worth, and though we often can't meet their expectations, at least they give us something to aim for.

Here lies the comfort as well as the ultimate flaw of our wizards' standards: They're based on our actions alone. And that framework gets everything backward. God did not create us as *human doers*. He created us as *human beings*.

Human doers derive identity from what they accomplish and the trophies they get, while *human beings* derive identity from knowing who they are despite what they accomplish or what happens to them. Humanity controls the standard—and the deception—for what it means to be the greatest *human doer*, while Adonai alone controls what it means to be *human beings*.

Seeking value from a wizard gives us the wrong information because wizards root our worth in performance. This dynamic sets us up for a lifetime of exhaustion and disappointment. Performance requires constant work in order to maintain the approval and acceptance of a person or group. At some point, you're going to drop the ball. The facade will crumble. All that work, and there you are, totally defeated. You could spend your life toggling back and forth, either drowning in work to prove you're enough or wallowing in despair because the bottom has dropped out and you feel like a loser.

Instead of falling into the cycle of proving yourself through what you do, ask your Maker to reveal who you are and, with that, the full scope of your value and the potential choices you can make when you begin to exercise your agency.

When you have that, you're one step closer to transformation.

LIE 3: YOU CAN FIND ALL THE ANSWERS WITHIN YOURSELF.

Society would have us believe that we are fully autonomous beings, that all the answers are found only within ourselves. That the *only* thing we need to reach our full potential is confidence in ourselves. Do we honestly have the ability to self-generate the courage to change? And is that really all it takes?

This is a very potent lie, primarily because it's so close to the truth. Yes, God has made you the way you are for a reason. He made you to be yourself—but he didn't make you to be *by* yourself. We will discuss this more in the coming chapters, but for now, know that transformation doesn't happen in isolation. You don't just need confidence *in yourself* and *by yourself*. Growth and change come through the power of our Creator applied within the wisdom of a community. Remember, we're better together.

If you assume that you have everything you need within yourself, you are likely to try going it alone, without the proper support of a community. When that happens, you're almost certain to crash and burn. After you've failed to meet the expectations you've set for yourself, when you're feeling disappointed and inadequate, you're in the perfect position to turn to a wizard—someone who claims he or she alone can fix you.

Yes, it's true that you don't have all the answers within yourself. You need others. But here's an important distinction: You need others—*plural*. Not just one other person. When you shape your whole life around the advice of just one other person, allowing that person and that person only to guide and shape the way you think and behave, that person becomes a wizard in your life. Hence the need for a multitude of counselors.

This is not to say that you bear no sense of personal responsibility, that what you think isn't important, or that self-confidence doesn't matter at all. Feelings often do make a difference in how we behave. But self-confidence generally builds *after* we've found the courage to make a well-informed decision. And that courage is best fostered in a loving community—not through striking out on your own.

And if you still feel you lack the courage to begin, don't worry. As we move from desperation to transformation, we will all feel alternately victorious and defeated, encouraged and discouraged, enlightened and ignorant, as we stride boldly or stumble forward. Along the way, we will meet with both the brave and the poor in spirit, but let's remember which group is promised the kingdom.[4]

MEET YOUR MAKER

If there's anyone who demonstrated being both brave and poor in spirit, it was young David when we first meet him in the Old Testament. In 1 Samuel 17, we see David face his own wizard moment. God had put power beyond imagining at his disposal. By the time we meet David in this chapter, he had already proved his strength: He had killed lions and bears with his own hands. He had no need to seek help from man. King Saul, however, attempted to establish himself as a wizard in David's life.

When David volunteered to square up with Goliath, Saul insisted that David wear the king's armor. Perhaps Saul assumed that the armor's inherent value as the possession of a king would lend David strength—strength he'd already proven he didn't need. David, however, knew what he really needed—and it wasn't flashy armor from a king. It was God.[5]

Only your Maker sees who you really are. He knew you before you were conceived, he sees your current situation, and he fully comprehends your future. As the One who brought you into existence, sustains you through life, and ushers you into eternity, God has information no wizard can ever access. He knows who you are, what he created you to be, and what it'll take to awaken a better you. As he did with David, God gives us exactly what we need. In David's case, it was five smooth stones and instructions for how to disrupt Israel's current paradigm. In our case, it's a list of saints who have gone before and can show us how to escape the wizard's tangled web of lies.

BLESSED ARE THE DISRUPTERS

God sees the lies that lead us to wizards. That's why from time to time, he sees fit to bless us with disrupters to show us how to break free. These iconoclasts burst out of desperate situations, shatter society's expectations, and bring powerful change to the very systems set to define them. They show us that no matter when you're born, what systems seek to hold you down, or who is against you, you have the power to disrupt.

- With her speech "Ain't I a Woman?" Sojourner Truth disrupted America's distorted ideas of both Blackness and womanhood.

- By adopting a girl from a lower-level caste, Mahatma Gandhi disrupted India's rigid social hierarchy and launched a global nonviolent movement of civil disobedience.
- Clearly articulating the lived experience of the oppressed, Martin Luther King, Jr., disrupted America's century-long caste system that was hiding in systematic segregation.
- Firmly committed to giving voice to the silenced, Fannie Lou Hamer disrupted organized structures of American voter repression.
- The ultimate disrupter, Yeshua of Nazareth dissected space and time, coming as God in the flesh to disrupt Satan's ongoing deception of humanity and his long assault against the throne of Yahweh.

We think of these disrupters as heroic, yet in many ways they were just ordinary people (with the exception of Yeshua) who knew their value and worked to help others recover value for themselves. Out of their desperation, they made decisions very similar to the one I made in sixth grade. They decided not to let their circumstances define them. Instead, they flipped the script. Each in their own way dethroned wizards.

DETHRONING THE WIZARDS

A wizard's real power takes root in great insecurity—when you don't believe in yourself and the beauty of the way your Creator made you. But when you see that you no longer need the magic of the wizard to transform, their power over you is broken.

Dethroning wizards can be terrifying because we're unsure if we are enough. You are. God has blessed you with gifts, powers, skills, and unique abilities. You may not have realized yet that you have access to them. You may be overlooking their value. Like Dorothy with her slippers, you may not even feel like you want them! Society seeks to stack the deck against us. We believe the lies. People cause us to doubt ourselves, and the circumstances of life often reinforce those doubts. When that happens, we wind up taking a page out of Dorothy's book, denying the value of the very things we own that could liberate us.

Dorothy and her friends didn't need to visit the Wiz to succeed. Neither do you. (Although if visiting the Wiz meant hanging with Michael Jackson, I'd have given it some thought.) In the end, it wasn't a wizard who actually changed them—it was the journey. It was an unlearning of inaccurate information and a relearning of the truth. It was a decision to exercise agency with newfound knowledge.

You can do this—even in the midst of your fear. You don't have to wait for the fear to vanish. Take the next step and watch what happens. Exercising agency diminishes fear because when you start seeing wins, your confidence grows. But it starts with making a choice to dethrone the wizards in your life.

You'll know you're on the right path when you're able to make your own decisions and practice your agency. When you exercise your own unique giftedness with confidence and skill, the wizards automatically lose their allure—and with it, their sway over you.

> **You can do this—even in the midst of your fear.**

Most wizards won't just leave. They must be driven out. Occasionally, however, wizards cannot be completely removed. If your spouse has become a wizard in your life, your solution is not to get rid of your spouse. The same could be said of a parent, a ministry partner, or a respected mentor. In some cases, instead of removing that person from your life, you must seek to put them in their proper place. Learn how to recognize the beauty of who you are and tap into your unique power. Step into your agency and dethrone your wizards.

FREE TO BE YOURSELF

When you realize that your value is not found in anyone else's estimation of you—rather, it flows directly from the hand of the Creator—you're truly free to be yourself. You can celebrate what makes you unique and special without feeling the need to seek constant external validation. When you're no longer comparing yourself to others but are looking to your Creator instead, you realize you already have everything you need to transform in mind, body, and spirit. Rather than seeking validation by trying to meet shifting societal or relational expectations, you can exercise your agency to identify, cultivate, and put to use your unique skills, gifts, and position in the world.

Remember, only *you* can be *you*. Your goal is not to change who you are to fit someone else's mold but to awaken a better version of who you already are. Your awakening may be starting right now, but it will last a lifetime. It's hard and sometimes scary, but it's worth it. It's worth it to know God and know yourself as seen through his eyes, to become the person your Creator has truly created you to be.

TALK IT OUT

1. Think of a time when you went to a wizard instead of to your Creator. What happened? What were the results? What advice would you offer based on that experience?
2. How can you guard against the tendency to seek value from wizards?

3. Which of the lies listed in this chapter are you most prone to believe? How does that lie drive you toward a wizard?

WORK IT OUT

What are some specific lies about yourself that you have been tempted to believe in the past or may be believing now?

How might these lies be hindering you?

What truths can you use to combat them?

Read this list of potential wizards in your life. Check the ones that might pose a danger for you. Fill in the blanks with any additional wizards you can identify.

☐ parent   ☐ ministry partners
☐ spouse/romantic partner   ☐ church family
☐ children/dependents   ☐ _____
☐ friend   ☐ _____
☐ boss   ☐ _____
☐ co-workers   ☐ _____
☐ pastor/church leaders   ☐ _____

WRITE IT OUT

Spend five minutes freewriting about your wizards: the ones you find most alluring, the emptiness of their promises, and how they've failed you in the past. Brainstorm steps you might take toward dethroning your wizards.

PART TWO

How to Build a
Better You

Now that you have a firm understanding of who you are and you know how to watch for those things that can hinder growth and strip you of your agency, you can move forward to awakening a better you in four interconnected areas: your mind and emotions, your physical self, your relationships with others, and your spirit. In the chapters to come, we will break these areas down one by one.

As you grow in these areas, you will move through what I like to call the four steps of transformation: desperation, information, application, and transformation. These four steps will be present in every single one of your growth areas. Learning how the process works and understanding each step along the way is vital to intentional, lasting transformation.

DESPERATION

Identify a problem you desperately want to change.

While it's true you seek to awaken a better self as a whole—mind, body, and spirit—it's also true that desperation in at least one specific area of your life will create the motivation to get the ball rolling.

- A health crisis in your own life or the life of a family member or friend pushes you to take your relationship with your body seriously.

- A mental or emotional crisis forces you to recognize the depths of your trauma.
- A relational crisis uncovers your need for stronger systems around relationships.
- A spiritual crisis causes you to strengthen your faith foundations.

Sometimes you're hit from multiple angles at the same time. Whatever problem you've identified, you can experience significant change when you make a conscious decision to move past desperation to seek the right information.

INFORMATION

Research the problem, unlearn built-in ideas, and vet data through proof of concept.

The internet has given us access to more information than we could possibly handle. In some ways, though, this free access has only served to muddy the waters. Within seconds, search engines can give us access to trending articles and video content from self-styled influencers ready to instruct us on everything from how to get out of debt to how to raise our children or finally find love. This ease of access can not only make us intellectually lazy but also prove misleading. Internet searches point out popular answers, but there's no guarantee they are the right answers—particularly for you.

Any data you discover on your quest for information must be vetted through proof of concept. That means you must intentionally seek experienced coaches, mentors, and guides who can cut through the chatter and speak with authority from personal experience. Make sure they're ahead of you, down the road in whichever area you're seeking to develop (and, as we discussed in the previous chapter, not taking the role of a wizard in your life).

Whatever your needs, find experts who are experienced in the actual disciplines to walk with you and hold you accountable. They'll give you the right information for you and help you apply it in practical ways.

APPLICATION

Build a practical plan and take active steps to make the change.

Transformation doesn't happen by accident. It's always the result of intentional action guided by a well-ordered plan. With your chosen guide by your side, move from information to application by designing a practical plan with reasonable steps to walk the path toward transformation. Remember, depending on where you are and where you wish to go, what these steps look like, the order in which you take them, and the amount of time it takes to accomplish each one will always vary. Never compare your journey of transformation with another person's. When you stand before God one day and give an account of your life, you will not be responsible for the choices others have made—but you will have to give an account of your own. There could be no greater motivation than that to take steps toward awakening a better you.

> **Transformation is always the result of intentional action guided by a well-ordered plan.**

TRANSFORMATION

Celebrate as change happens and embrace a mindset of continual growth.

In many ways, transformation is more a process that you will engage throughout your entire life than it is a single event. As you actively take steps to transform, your efforts will be rewarded with tangible results. Those positive results will fuel even more change.

It's important that along the way you take time to celebrate when change happens, sharing your joy with your guides, family members, friends, and surrounding community. While growth does benefit you, it isn't just for you. When you awaken a better you, we all become a better us. That's definitely worth celebrating.

TRANSFORMATION IN ACTION: CARYL REID

Caryl Reid was at an impasse.

His life didn't seem to be going anywhere. It's not that he was lazy. If a goal was set for him, he reached it. He graduated from college, found a career, and served in ministry. Despite these achievements, Caryl still felt dissatisfied.

"There were other things I wanted to do but wasn't given the guide or permission to pursue them."

Looking around, he saw others making progress, pursuing passions, and collecting wins. Caryl would outwardly celebrate their success. Inwardly, he envied their progress.

He hated this cycle, yet he felt trapped in it. Caryl knew that instead of looking at other people's lives and feeling sorry for himself, he needed to focus more on his own life. He wanted to establish his own goals and create a plan for how he would accomplish them.

That brought Caryl to me.

In our life-coaching sessions, I challenged Caryl to identify the areas of his life in which he wanted to experience growth. Targeting those areas, he created SMART—specific, measurable, attainable, realistic, time-based—goals that would help him move forward in practical and achievable ways.

Next, he began evaluating the media he consumed. Caryl adjusted his approach to ensure that what he was taking in was not only worth being consumed but also contained the information he needed to reach the next stage of his life. As a result, he began reading books and listening to podcasts that would help him form habits focused on holistic wellness.

Caryl also began to seek out and build relationships with people who could serve as mentors. He believes this was key to his transformation. "Even though I was gaining the right information, I needed the support of people who were familiar with the position I was in, knew how to apply the information I had gained, and could hold me accountable to following through."

Caryl began connecting with others who were either in the same phase of development or had already embarked in the direction he was headed. These relationships kept him on the right path and encouraged him along the way.

When he found a helpful book, Caryl would join a book club in which like-minded people discussed their successes and challenges in applying the information. He also became more intentional about scheduling meetups and holding regular conversations with men who could advise him in the areas he'd targeted for growth. They would check in with him to see how he had been doing in achieving his goals. For more pressing matters, he sought guidance through therapy and prayer.

The first and most important transformation Caryl recognized was in his self-image. His understanding of who he was and what he could do was no longer rooted in self-deprecation but in self-affirmation.

"I embraced that I am still loved and lovable even though I am flawed and prone to making mistakes. I learned to celebrate who I was and grow in understanding who I am as a believer and a builder."

Caryl also witnessed a transformation in his appearance. He

> "I am still loved and lovable even though I am flawed and prone to making mistakes."

participated in programs like the "45-Day Challenge" at Build a Better Us, engaged with a community that made a commitment to improving their holistic health, and learned from personal trainers and nutritionists, all of which led to an improvement in both his physique and his physical health.

He also enjoyed an improved social life, due largely to his mindset shift in how he approached relationships. Understanding that every relationship must be approached as an investment, Caryl no longer maintained close connections with people who simply made withdrawals of his time and advice without contributing anything in return. Instead, he chose to focus on bonds with those who reciprocated and strengthened him in turn.

Caryl's transformation doesn't just benefit him, however. With his new approach to life, everyone around him reaps the rewards. He said, "I believe that my transformation led my surrounding community to have more conversations and create actionable steps for improving their own health and wellness. I've been able to host conversations about mental health among the youth in my community as well as incorporate strategies in my classroom that would cultivate their mental health, such as journaling, breaks for physical activity, and sharing their feelings and challenges with their peers. I have also been able to coach and support others in their journey to physical health as I would engage in discussion about their diet and exercise routine and offer suggestions for actionable steps."

From envious to inspiring, from feeling stuck to pressing forward, from needing care to caring for the community—this is the essence of awakening a better you.

TALK IT OUT

1. Where did you see the transformation steps in Caryl's story? Which of the four transformation steps caught your attention and why?

2. How did the four growth points (mental/emotional, physical, relational, spiritual) in Caryl's story connect and overlap? How can seeking development in one area automatically help in other areas? Discuss examples of how this might work in your own life.

3. Which growth points have traditionally been overlooked in your community? Which ones have been emphasized—or perhaps overemphasized to the neglect of others? What were the effects of this dynamic?

WORK IT OUT

Flip back to page 13 where you ranked your growth areas. Have your priorities changed? If so, which of the four growth areas do you suspect will be the one(s) you will need to address? If not, re-write your top area of growth in the space below.

When you think about that growth area, which transformation step (desperation, information, application, transformation) do you think you're currently in?

What challenges do you anticipate facing?

What steps can you take to face those challenges?

WRITE IT OUT

Spend five minutes freewriting about the four growth points. List out what an integrated approach toward holistic growth and development might look like for you.

5

Awaken a Better Mental and Emotional You

When I was six years old and my brother Joe was two, I saved his life for the first time. We were living in South Dallas. My parents, sister, brother, and I shared a one-bedroom apartment on the second floor. I was playing a game I'd learned from some of the older boys from our complex. We would run around the building, sprint up the stairs to the very top, turn around, shimmy backward through the rails, drop our bodies down, and grip the supporting pole with our legs before sliding down like a firefighter leaving the fire station. Then we'd repeat the process—the faster the better.

One day, my little brother Joe tried to follow us. He ran up the stairs, shimmied backward through the rails, but was too small to reach the pole. There he dangled, twenty feet in the air, silhouetted against the sky, a breath from death—stomach to the concrete, little hands gripping, tiny legs flailing.

I had to save him. I dashed up the steps, dropped to the ground, and reached through the poles. I grabbed Joe's little body and held on for dear life. I didn't have the strength to pull him up—I only had enough strength not to let him go.

Our neighbors saw what was happening and began gathering below, shouting, their sober gazes fixed on us. "Drop him! We'll catch him!" Yeah, right. I didn't care who was down there. I wasn't letting my brother go.

My four-year-old sister, Rachel, heard everything and ran to find our parents. They rushed out and helped drag Joe back over the side. My mother was frantic, in disbelief, still panicking though the danger had passed. I understood how she felt. I just kept repeating, "I would not let him go. I would not let him go."

Even if that had been the only time I saved my brother's life, it would have been enough to make a deep impression on me. But it wasn't the only time—not by a long shot. When I was in my first drive-by shooting at eleven years old, my brother Joe was there. I dove on top of him as bullets flew over our heads at the park. When I almost got into a huge fight with thirty guys, Joe was there. He was also with me at the state fair in Dallas when rival gangs were beefing with each other at a riot with thousands of other people.

Every year, the Dallas Independent School District booked a night at the fair for their students. It was a day of eating cotton candy and turkey, getting numbers from the opposite sex, and witnessing the inevitable gang fights. Like clockwork, every time we went, people would be pepper sprayed, stabbed, and trampled. It was kind of the grand finale. The Dallas police were ready for this, of course, with rubber bullets, tear gas, and horses.

That year, I was sixteen. Joe was twelve. We were together when it all popped off. Neither of us saw how it started, but things went from zero to sixty in a second. People were running, screaming— it was literal mayhem. We took off sprinting, Joe and me. When we paused at a side street, we heard gunshots. Turning toward the sound, I looked over and saw a girl trip and land flat on her face, busting it wide open. She lifted her hands to her mouth—

they came away bloody. I made eye contact with Joe. Time to take charge. "We have got to go *now*."

I wasn't sure what to do, but I knew I had to fix it. There was no other choice. I was the responsible older sibling. Joe's life was in my hands. I had to save him—and I did. The moment of danger passed, and yet it never really did. In some ways it never will. I didn't know it then, but that's how trauma works. It stretches the pain and fear of these moments to encompass our entire lives.

MIND PLAYING TRICKS ON ME

Mental health was never something we talked about when I was growing up. There weren't any pills or evaluations. If you acted up, it wasn't because you were traumatized. You were just "bad." You were either paddled at school, beat by your parents, put in special education, or put on a track from school to prison. We always joked about little White kids in the suburbs acting out and their parents giving them Ritalin instead of disciplining them. We had no idea how the brain worked. We just knew it was "bad" to get in trouble.

The closest we got to mental health education was when rap artists Geto Boys dropped a song called "Mind Playing Tricks on Me," in which they described how individuals were seemingly having psychotic episodes because something was wrong with their minds. Bushwick Bill sang about his hands being bloody from punching concrete. That made sense to me. It described the world I knew.

No one ever talked about how trauma literally reshapes our brains and bodies.[1] Or how researchers discovered that people who have a long history of trauma actually develop a disproportionate number of diagnosable medical conditions, including chronic pain and autoimmune disorders.

No one talked about how trauma would affect us not just physically but emotionally, causing ripple effects through all our relationships. That we would struggle in our adult friendships and marriages. That we would grapple with ongoing nightmares, anxiety, and depression. That every once in a while, we'd just stop functioning in relationships, having literally woken up one morning feeling frozen, suddenly and overwhelmingly unable to cope with our own lives. Because even if we hadn't yet paused to soberly process our trauma, our brains and bodies were still keeping score.[2]

For decades, I lived side by side with the ongoing desperation of unresolved personal and communal trauma. I couldn't move past it because (1) I didn't have the right information to understand the brain and (2) I didn't know what applications could help me heal. Maybe that describes you too.

Learning to recognize trauma, understanding how it affects you, and seeking healing are some of the best steps you can take toward transformation. To move forward, we first need to understand how our complex brains work.

THE COMPLEX BRAIN

In some ways, your mind works like the internet does. Once something's on the internet, it's out there forever. In a similar way, once a memory is filed in your brain, it's in there for life. Though things get pushed down and covered over, once an event gets filed in your memory bank, it never truly goes away. This is especially true of traumatic memories, which mess with the brain's smoothly running filing system.

The Brain's Filing System

In the 2003 film *Bruce Almighty*, a man named Bruce, played by Jim Carrey, complains about how God is running the world. Shortly thereafter, he's contacted by God, played by Morgan Freeman, who is dressed in an impeccable white suit. When God lets on that he knows facts and details about Bruce's life, Bruce asks how he knows those things. God points at a small white filing cabinet, telling Bruce that everything he's ever said, done, or thought about doing has been recorded and stored in the files. When Bruce opens the filing cabinet, he is launched across the warehouse by a seemingly infinite drawer.

Your brain's filing system rests in the hippocampus and is a lot like that filing cabinet. Imagine you have a filing cabinet in your skull. It organizes thoughts and monitors learning and memory loops. Every time you have a new experience, the mind opens its filing cabinet and drops in a file. Walk to the store? Drop in a file. Read an email? Drop in a file. Watch a funny video on YouTube? Drop in a file. See anything by Dave Chappelle? Files on files.

The files sit there, neatly stored in the hippocampus, ready to be pulled out at a moment's notice to add vital context to a story and inform your understanding of the world, be it fear, sadness, joy, humor, or inspiration. Why? Because the hippocampus doesn't work alone. It tag-teams with the amygdala.

Think of the hippocampus as the home of your thoughts and the amygdala as the home of your feelings. As part of the brain's limbic system, the amygdala plays a key role in handling emotions, especially ones related to memory. Whenever your brain stores a new experience or pulls out an existing file, the amygdala slaps on an emoji. So, working together, the amygdala and the hippocampus regulate your memories and related emotional responses.[3]

The relationship between these two parts of the brain explains why what you see, hear, or smell can trigger such profound memories. Don't believe it? Close your eyes and imagine biting into a sour pickle or drinking pure lemon juice. If your mouth is watering, that's because the file associated with those memories is causing it to.

Every time your brain is given an external prompt, it goes into its filing cabinet and pulls out what it feels is an appropriate response. Sometimes, the brain pulls out a warm, fuzzy feeling, like when you taste cold water from a water hose and are instantly transported back to the endless summer days of childhood. The way the brain's filing system works also explains why one whiff of a school cafeteria makes you break out in a cold sweat and why the sound of a barking dog pumps you with adrenaline.

The call-and-response system held in place by the hippocampus and amygdala works well enough, all things considered. But like any system, it can be corrupted.

Trauma corrupts the files.

Corrupted Files

When trauma occurs, the hippocampus still adds information to your filing cabinet like it's supposed to. After all, that's what the hippocampus *does*. Since it acts as your memory bank, it must store the information related to the traumatic event. But a traumatic memory doesn't fit neatly in the drawers like a regular file does.

For the brain, filing trauma is much like trying to file a beach ball. Distorted, bloated, and unfit for the space provided, traumatic memories don't slide neatly into the filing cabinet of the mind. The hippocampus still tries to do its job and stuffs the memory in there, but though the memory is "filed," it doesn't function like a regular memory. Instead of remaining quietly in its place, it bounces around, noisy and disruptive. And to make it even more challenging, you can't access it the way you would a regular memory because it's a corrupted file. It doesn't stay put. You may sense it in there somewhere, rolling around and making noise, but when you reach for it, you find it eludes you.

Here's where things get tricky. While the memory itself remains a "corrupted file," the related emotional responses are still fully accessible.[4] That means that though the memory is not easy for you to connect with, the emotions are still fully there, bouncing around in the background like a Harlem Globetrotter playing keep-away. As you can imagine, this dynamic creates unpredictable responses.

Long-Term Storage

This is what happened with my memories associated with my little brother. Every time I witnessed Joe having a brush with death, the memories were filed away in my mind along with an emotional response. But these were corrupted files. Though I rarely thought about them and the sharp edges of reality blunted them over time, the quiet fear never went away. The terror simmered in the back of my mind, boring channels deep into my subconscious, ready to burst forth at unexpected moments—such as a wedding.

When my brother walked down the aisle to marry his wife— while everyone else was rejoicing in celebration—I had a meltdown. The moment Joe stepped out with his groomsmen, the deep well of emotion boiled over, and I began to sob uncontrollably. I know the DJ thought he was killing 'em with the Stevie Wonder playlist, but all I could think was that my brother could have died—that I'd almost let him go. What if he had fallen from the second story that day? What if I hadn't pushed him down fast enough when the bullets were flying? What if we hadn't escaped that riot at the fair? What if he'd died in my arms?

On Joe's wedding day, the link between my childhood memories and my emotional state was obvious, even to me. What I hadn't grasped was how those same memories had been driving my subconscious response to other aspects of my life, ones seemingly unrelated to Joe. The roiling inner panic of unprocessed trauma subtly colored my entire worldview, ratcheting up the tension in otherwise ordinary situations and constantly raising the stakes to the level of life and death. This was clearly unresolved trauma at work. Only I couldn't see it for what it was.

UNRESOLVED TRAUMA

The way you experience your trauma is the way a fish experiences water. To the fish, being under water feels totally natural. *Good,* even. He's a fish, and he's meant to swim in water.

If a passerby were to walk around the lake and call down, "How's the water?" the fish would look up, confused. "What's water?"

What water is to a fish, unresolved trauma is to people who haven't soberly processed their lives: totally encompassing, yet strangely invisible. Why is it so difficult to recognize unresolved trauma as a driving force behind our choices?

First, many of us don't take enough time to pause and reflect or practice introspection. We experience trauma but press forward as if nothing that's happened in the past will affect our present. Instead of slowing down to ask why we behave the way we do, we allow a quick pace of life, apathy, and a lack of desire to stir up painful memories that derail our progress.

There's also something to be said for the power of habit. Our habitual behaviors create deep grooves in our brains, and patterns become entrenched. What you originally did to protect yourself in the past has now become an unexamined matter of course. Your coping mechanisms are now routine. Your experience feels normative. Over time, you forget how you got to this point—you even forget that not everyone feels like you do or responds to life in the same way. For you, this is just how it feels to be a person. This is your pond. A fish was made to swim in water, but you were not designed to swim in trauma.

HOW WE GOT HERE

How do you wind up swimming in a sea of trauma? During some vulnerable point in your past, someone or something hurt you deeply. It didn't have to be loud or earth-shattering—trauma can enter quietly, sometimes in total silence. Either way, that experience now subtly shapes your entire life, often without analysis or permission:

- Emotional pain leads to numb feelings.
- Past abuse results in being overly self-protective.
- Feeling neglected or unseen prompts voluntary overexposure.
- Exploitation fosters a future unwillingness to be known, seen, or truthful.
- Church hurt causes intentional isolation from vital spiritual connection.
- Relational pain generates distrust and creates a deep sense of loneliness.

Unfortunately, that list could go on. If these traumas are left unchecked, the patterns of living that flow from them will only become more deeply entrenched.

Further compounding matters, people seeking to manage emotional chaos in the wake of unprocessed trauma often resort to harmful coping mechanisms. Sex, alcohol, substances, stonewalling, anger—these tactics offer a temporary escape from the pain. But the relief only lasts so long. In the long run, fallout from coping mechanisms not only further complicates your life but can also keep you from recognizing the warning signs of an approaching personal breakdown.

THE PATTERN

Looking back now, I recognize a pattern. Throughout my teen years and into young adulthood, whenever I saw a problem, I leaped to resolve it, convincing myself that if I didn't act, someone would die. That is kind of why I'm writing this book and how my career as a life coach chose me. When my friends and I began marrying and starting families, I observed that we were all grappling with supporting our children while trying to keep our relationships alive, and I felt the need for immediate response. If I didn't help them, if I didn't act, if I didn't do something, someone would die.

So, I went from knowing nothing about helping individuals, couples, and families to developing processes and systems to help them thrive. I founded Build a Better Us and began speaking into people's lives. I developed other coaches and brought them on board so that we could help as many people in as many ways as possible. This wasn't simply a career move for me. It was something I realized I *had* to do. To me, the stakes were life and death.

But though I was helping others, I still hadn't learned to help myself. Read that again. When it came to healing from trauma, I had moved from desperation to seeking information. I'd even started sharing that information with others. But I needed to learn

> There's a lot more to healing than simply "moving on."

how to apply that information to heal from my trauma and push forward to awaken a better me. And take note: There's a lot more to healing than simply "moving on."

THE MYTH OF MOVING ON

Maturing from childhood to adulthood comes with some major letdowns. You learn that staying up as late as you want isn't all it's cracked up to be. Laundry doesn't fold itself. The fridge doesn't magically fill up with food. Adulting isn't for the faint of heart.

Perhaps the most shocking part of adulthood is the way in which it shatters the myth of "moving on." Most of us came of age believing our friendships, marriages, and careers would somehow move us beyond the problems of our past. That time would distance us from our trauma. That success in these areas would heal the loneliness and cure the pain from an absent parent or a painful relationship. Instead, we've found that the weight that comes with adult responsibilities only further reveals our brokenness and can lead to unexpected breakdowns that are triggered by present circumstances but rooted in past trauma.

Most of us assumed that by this point in our lives, we'd have it more together. We'd have more answers, fewer disasters, and a better understanding of why we act the way we do. Yet here we are, full-grown adults, still making it up as we go.

Some of these struggles are inevitable. The world is full of darkness, and life is hard. At the bottom of it all, bouncing around like a stray ball, complicating every other issue we face, is our unresolved trauma. Until we deal with that, we'll never really "move on." We'll just keep rotating through a never-ending trauma spiral. To stop the spiral, you must face your unprocessed trauma.

UNLABELED STORAGE

When I was growing up, my mother kept countless boxes in the garage that couldn't be thrown away because one day we'd "need them." Maybe you recognize this urge. You probably have at least one box in your house that you haven't opened in years. You might have a vague idea of what's in there: trophies, pictures (from back when we actually printed things out), a childhood stuffed animal, love letters from an ex. You really should sort through it and decide what to keep and what to throw away, but the process sounds too tiring. It seems easier just to keep a lid on everything for now.

You may be taking a similar approach with your past trauma. You've packed up the memories and squirreled them away. Sexual shame stuffed into the attic. Spiritual abuse shoved under the bed. Painful abandonment slipped into trunks and pushed into corners. You pile other memories on top, praying the dust will cover everything like a blanket.

But life interferes. Contents shift during turbulence. Boxes burst open; feelings fly everywhere. One day you're seemingly fine. The next, you're a disaster. Hunched at your desk, hyperventilating. Waking in a cold sweat, shaking off nightmares. Sobbing uncontrollably in the shower. Relationships, accidents, seasons of life, injuries, fluctuating hormones—all these and more elicit emotions linked to traumas you'd hoped were safely packed away. But the boxes won't stay shut forever. You're forced either to deal with the contents or spiral into despair, your life completely taken over by coping mechanisms. Instead of waiting for your boxes to burst open, seek help to safely unpack them on your own terms.

MY JOE-SHAPED BOX

The source of my Joe-related trauma is obvious to me now. But for many years, I couldn't see it for what it was. That's because, for as many times as Joe had been in danger, he'd survived. The positive ending to each of these stories made me forget how much trauma I'd endured in the moment.

If my brother had actually died or suffered a terrible injury during any of our hood escapades, I may have connected the dots sooner. Since he survived, however, I didn't think of these moments as traumatic until years later during a bout with personal depression, when a friend, Adam Thomason, asked me to retell my life story. He asked me a simple question, "What's your birth order?" That was the first time I had considered how being the firstborn affected my extreme responses to my brother being in danger. In all those moments—the time he'd dangled from the railing, the time we'd almost been shot, the time we'd been in the stampede—I'd behaved as if it was my job (and mine alone) to keep my brother alive. Those experiences had traumatized me, leading me to believe that someone might die if I didn't act, and I carried that trauma into my present-day relationships.

Through Adam's guidance, I was able to process the right information and apply it to my situation, which helped me move past my feelings of desperation toward true healing. I can now explain how trauma has affected me in the past, how it's affecting me now, and how it may still affect me down the line. In order for you to heal from your trauma, you will need to move through a similar process. Then you can say that you've dealt with it and can begin moving toward mental and emotional transformation.

UNPACK THE BOXES

The first step toward this transformation is to identify the source of unprocessed trauma. Remember, trauma isn't necessarily the result of tragic, chaotic upheaval. Trauma can enter on cat's feet, sneaking in through the back door. It's also highly individualized and can result from anything disruptive that is specific to your experience. To anyone else, the trigger may sound like a small matter. But it isn't small for you.

You'll recognize trauma not necessarily by the explosiveness of the event but by the way it's created in you a new mode of experiencing the world. Unprocessed trauma can reveal itself when certain triggers lead you to respond in ways that seem disproportionate or irrational to others. Think of the moments when someone outside your family has observed your reaction and seemed totally shocked by something you do all the time, something that your family would take in stride. This outwardly illogical response is not illogical at all—it's the result of unresolved trauma. A fish-in-water moment. Although the situation may not merit an explosive response, the emoji attached to the memory is based on information no one else is privy to—perhaps not even you, if your trauma hasn't been recognized for what it is.

The good news (if we can call anything about this "good") is that you don't have to search hard for your traumas. The daily stresses of life are enough to reveal them. Often a crisis throws them into stark relief. You're laid off from a job. You move to a new city. A relationship falls apart. One way or another, no matter how carefully you've packed your traumas away, the boxes will eventually burst open. What's less certain is how you'll deal with the fallout.

When you notice a pattern of behavior (often linked to a disproportionate emotional response), ask yourself the following questions:

- *Where did this behavior come from?*
- *How long has it affected me?*
- *Is it affecting me in ways I haven't yet recognized?*

Depending on the levels of your trauma and your own self-awareness, asking these questions by yourself might not be sufficient. You may need to discuss them with a close friend, family member, mentor, counselor, support group, or professional therapist (more on that later). An indicator that you're successfully un-packing your boxes is that you can begin to explain what's happened to you and how it's shaped you—good or bad.

ASKING FOR HELP

During my time as a teen lifeguard, I gave swimming tests. It still amazes me how many times kids would jump confidently into the water and nearly drown. Sometimes they'd sink straight to the bottom, leaving a trail of bubbles. Then there were those who would splash around and flail. Though clearly struggling, they didn't call out for a friend or signal a lifeguard. By the time I dove in, they were already headed down. Why, if they didn't know how to swim, would they jump in the water in the first place? And why, if they knew their life was at stake, would they not call for help?

Maybe they'd seen people swimming on TV, figured it looked easy enough, and jumped in without fully comprehending the danger. Maybe they knew the danger, but the desire to fit in with their peers outweighed the shame they felt they would face if they didn't pass the swim test.

Beloved, when it comes to trauma recovery, there's no need to dive into the deep end alone, not sure if you will sink or swim. There's no reason to let your head slip silently beneath the water. You don't need to struggle alone. There's help available.

People who are drowning know they're in trouble, but they need trust and courage to call out and believe someone will re-spond to their cries. Maybe this describes you. People won't know what you need unless you tell them. Call out to God and others for help. Help is near, but you must give a sign. Lift your hand. Raise your voice. Open your mouth and say it aloud: "I need help." Whisper if you must. Shout if you can. We can read the signs. We can't read minds.

Your feelings matter, and you can ask for help. Asking for help is courageous. Let's be courageous.

HELP IS ON THE WAY

In our Creator's loving care, he has provided tools and resources to grapple with life's complexities. First, he's given us himself in the person and work of Yeshua. Additionally, he's bestowed us with Scripture, faith communities, and pastors to minister to our souls. But he didn't stop there. He's likewise gifted doctors, nurses, surgeons, nutritionists, and trainers to help care for our bodies. Mentors, counselors, and licensed therapists minister to the mind and emotions. Every day, our coaches at Build a Better Us lend their expertise in amazingly targeted ways, helping our BBU family learn, grow, heal, and transform.

Although many aspects of trauma recovery are interlocking, specific areas should always be treated in targeted ways by experts in those particular fields. Whatever area of your life you're working on, be sure you're following a suitable guide—someone who has vetted their advice through practical experience. Someone who can take you from a place of desperation, lead you to the right information, help you with application, and celebrate your transformation.

The person best suited to come alongside you will vary, depending on the types of issues you're facing. Some situations may call for pastoral counsel, but others require therapy. Some issues are psychological, some physiological, and some spiritual—this is why we need experienced guides. As I found out only after great struggle, you can't simply pray your way out of trauma. Fortunately, experts who are experienced in the disciplines related to your trauma can walk with you. They'll pinpoint the cause of your desperation, give you the right information, help you discover paths to application, and put you one step further down the road to transformation.

HOPE FOR THE HURTING

Perhaps this all sounds overwhelming. Rest assured that there's hope. Though the process of unpacking trauma may be difficult, there are both natural and supernatural resources available to help along the way.

Natural Reshaping

God wired you for change. He designed your brain for flexibility. This is what neurologists call *neuroplasticity,* a means by which both the structure and the function of your brain can be reshaped.[5] Experts who have studied this attribute of the brain explain that by unlearning entrenched thought processes, establishing new patterns of thinking, and forming new habits, brain maps can be rewritten.[6] In short, you can create a new normal. Because your Creator built your brain with neuroplasticity, you're able to form healthy new mind maps that alter not just the way you think but also the way you feel and behave as a result.

The bottom line? No one needs to stay stuck. Nothing is set in stone. Habits and patterns can change. You can change. No matter your levels of trauma or difficult past experiences, you can unpack your boxes, clean up the corrupted files, and become a stronger, more mature version of who you already are. Transformation is possible.

Supernatural Redemption

The steps above are important, but they are not ultimate. Identifying your unpacked boxes helps you know yourself. It helps you let the air out of those beach balls so that they fit into the filing cabinet better—still there, but quieter and not so prone to bouncing around and demanding attention. Real redemption doesn't come simply through natural processes, however. Real redemption comes when, through the process of trauma recovery, you experience the sufficiency of your God.

For me, healing from trauma began when I was able to unpack my boxes and understand why I respond to the world the way I do—believing that if I don't act, people will die. Trauma redemption came when I was able to hold those feelings up to the truth. The truth is, I do not hold the power of life and death in my hands. Instead of seeing my brother Joe's life (and the lives of my community) as my responsibility, I came to see that all our lives are in God's hands. I am not ultimately responsible for everyone's destiny. Only God is—and he knows how to make a way when there seems to be no way. This is the same lesson the patriarch Abraham learned.

When God called Abraham to take his son Isaac to sacrifice on Mount Moriah, Abraham obeyed. He assured his son that God would provide a lamb for the sacrifice—which he did. But the writer of Hebrews notes that during this event, Abraham grasped a deeper truth. Abraham also knew that even if Isaac died, God could raise the dead.[7]

I had to learn what Abraham did—that I am not ultimately responsible for life and death. Only my Creator is, and because he is worthy and good, I can trust him to do the work that I'm incapable of doing anyway. Though I still occasionally struggle with the feelings assigned to that corrupted file, God has redeemed my

> When trauma redemption happens, your trauma no longer defines you.
> It refines you.

pain by using it to show me his character and love in richer and deeper ways.

Trauma redemption comes only when you realize the truth about yourself *and* your God. When that happens, your trauma no longer defines you. It refines you. You'll no longer tell your story as victim but as a victor. Victory is possible. Victory is here.

TALK IT OUT

1. Think about the complexities of the brain. What surprised you about the hippocampus (filing system) and the amygdala (emoji stamps)?
2. How will understanding the relationship between memories and emotions impact how you interact with others in the future?
3. Describe a moment when a past hurt led you to a disproportionate emotional response. To what extent was trauma at the root of your reaction?
4. Why is asking for help important when dealing with unprocessed trauma?

WORK IT OUT

Repeat this sentence aloud: "My feelings matter."
List any feelings or emotional reactions that you can't explain to yourself:

What painful experiences from your past have you not yet dealt with in a serious and meaningful way?

How is your trauma primarily affecting you? In the following space, check all that apply. Under each area you've indicated, list any symptoms you have pinpointed as a result of that trauma. Then consider what you must choose to do (or do differently) in order to deal with your trauma.

☐ Spiritually

☐ Relationally

☐ Mentally

☐ Emotionally

☐ Physically

As you walk through unboxing your trauma, remember: Asking for help is courageous. Who will help you seek professional assistance and offer loving support?

List the steps you will take to seek care:

Step 1:

Step 2:

Step 3:

Step 4:

WRITE IT OUT

Spend five minutes freewriting about trauma, pain, and unpacking boxes. Brainstorm truths about God that speak to your particular pain and any further steps you might take toward trauma redemption.

6

Awaken a Better Physical You

In 2013 I was at a conference when my mother called me, sobbing, with the news of my father's unexpected death. He was only fifty-three. I remember the shock of that day.

Apart from the natural grief of a son for a beloved father, I was further shaken because he hadn't even been sick. Yes, he'd used tobacco products, worked long hours, drank energy drinks to stay awake, and ate fast food. But since he'd never been seriously ill, didn't use drugs, and wasn't overweight, we all thought he was fine. But his body and heart couldn't take it anymore.

My dad had been malnourished. Even though he lived in these United States of America in the twenty-first century and had eaten three meals a day, his body didn't have the nutrients it needed to survive. How did he not notice? Turns out, my dad hadn't felt the effects of malnourishment because he'd stayed full on fake food.

FOOD PLAYIN' TRICKS ON US

I came of age enjoying the same diet as my dad. I survived on cheeseburgers from the corner store, Little Debbie cakes, and Jungle Juice. Did you grow up with Jungle Juice? Cheap and delicious, it was the flavor of my childhood, and it cost only fifty cents at the corner store. You couldn't drink any without spilling it on yourself. I can still taste the tang on the back of my tongue and see the juice splotches on our school shirts.

Imagine my shock the first time I read the fine print on those little cartons and saw the words "Contains No Juice." How could a drink with *juice* in the name literally *contain no juice*? When you live in the hood, though, you are not looking for presentation, flavor, and nutritious ingredients so much as what will take up space in your stomach and stop the hunger pains. Living in the hood meant we walked to the corner store for chicken wings, fries, and whatever else was cheap and fast. We ate whatever we could get our hands on to stay full. You know you're in survival mode when you crack open a can of meat and have to scrape the jelly off.

Even after we moved to a slightly better neighborhood, our fridge was filled with bologna, hot dogs, and anything else that was cheap and would feed a family. Momma would literally make miracles in the kitchen with random items.

One of my favorite childhood memories was when my dad would wake my entire family up at 2 A.M. to eat Whataburger. For over twenty years, my father worked twelve to sixteen hours a day in a freight yard to provide for us. When he got home on Friday nights, we'd wake up in the dead of night and line up against the wall. He'd walk down the hall handing out warm paper-wrapped burgers, sticky with cheese and slippery with oil. My stomach aches at the thought of eating a cheeseburger and fries at 2 A.M. now, but when I was a kid? Man—what kid wouldn't love that?

But what my dad thought was keeping us alive was literally killing him. He was unaware of how our survival relationship with food affected our overall health, and he unknowingly passed these habits down to me, the next generation. It wasn't until my dad passed that I experienced a desperation strong enough to drive me to soberly consider that a poor relationship with food could have grave consequences.

AN UNINFORMED APPROACH

Before my father's death, I had tried to make productive, healthy changes. I had sensed some sort of need for better self-care, but I didn't possess enough information to make a permanent change.

During my and Vanja's first year of marriage, my weight started to fluctuate. Regular BJ and thick BJ. At first, it didn't seem like a big deal because I could always lose it after feeling a little shame. Everyone who gets married gains weight, right? (Marrieds, I see you looking cute, acting like it didn't happen to you.) Though I shrugged off the weight gain at first, eventually it really became an issue. I gained roughly twenty pounds in less than a year. I began wondering, *What am I doing? What if the trend continues?* This was not okay.

Now, I'll be the first to acknowledge that there are lots of reasons why people gain weight that have nothing to do with poor eating habits. But that wasn't the case for me. I was discontent with my body, my clothes didn't fit, and I knew it was because I wasn't taking care of myself. Alarmed at how fast I was packing on the pounds, I decided to start working out.

In my mind, working out would solve my weight problem. That's how it works, right? I logged time in the gym and took up running. In reality, however, I had just jumped on a seesaw. I would work out; my weight would decrease. I would stop my workout binges; the weight would come back. And I still wasn't healthy.

A decade later, I was still riding the seesaw. I needed a new approach. Tired of weight fluctuations and low energy, I decided that the best way to get healthy was to cut out the stuff I really enjoyed: fried foods and sweets. Without taking the time to become truly informed about food, I simply decided to say good-bye to fried chicken, potato chips, donuts, and cake. All that and I still didn't see a significant change to my health. I was about to give up.

PERMANENT CHANGE

Around the time I realized that my drastic, no-fun diet wasn't cutting it, a friend of mine underwent surgery to correct some breathing issues. Before surgery, he hadn't been able to breathe well enough to be active. He was in ministry, basically lived an inactive life, and gained about a hundred pounds over a few years.

Post-surgery, he began to eat a plant-based diet. Everyone in our circles found this very strange. No one around us had ever chosen this sort of lifestyle, but I remember him saying, "All I know is when I do it, I feel better." Over the course of the next few months, he began losing serious weight. We're talking twenty, thirty, forty, and fifty pounds. As the weight dropped, he was able to increase his activity levels, and the progress just kept rolling. Our community watched as our friend created a whole new life for himself, and we rejoiced in his transformation.

Although I was happy for him, I thought he was being too extreme. My sentiment was, "You have fun eating your lil' plant-based diet. I'll be over here with my bacon and fries." And my twenty extra pounds. And my low energy. I'm not sure why, but I wasn't struck by the cognitive dissonance. My friend had found something that helped him stay healthy and keep thriving, while I was unhealthy and surviving. My temporary fixes had never ultimately worked, yet his application of informed changes had led to transformation.

CRITICAL OBSERVATION

Shortly after my friend's surgery, my son's elementary school put on a presentation centering on diet and food. Like any supportive father, I showed up, bracing myself to endure whatever cheesy presentation the kids had put together. No matter how cornball school events tend to be, I would stick it out for my son's sake. Or so I thought.

This presentation was on another level. When we walked in the door, the first thing I had to do was take a survey on a tablet, clicking on the choice that best represented my current diet:

- conventional—completely open with no restrictions or limitations on consumption
- vegetarian—abstains from meat or meat by-products resulting from animal slaughter
- vegan—abstains from meat and all animal products and by-products
- pescatarian—largely vegetarian but includes eggs, dairy, fish, and seafood

Next, we walked through the exhibit, moving from station to station. As we progressed, the students demonstrated what a plate of food would look like and what nutrients we would be gaining based on our current diets. The truth bomb detonated: The diet I currently followed was the one with the least physical benefits.

What I'd missed in my childhood experiences and shied away from during my young adult life, this visual children's presentation made unavoidably obvious. I was keeping my belly full but not keeping my body nourished. Though I'd been putting lots of effort into "getting healthy" and had made some short-term changes to reach observable goals, I'd never bothered to become informed about food. I was placing my faith in conventional wisdom that I'd never investigated for myself.

TRANSFORMATION

At the beginning of the following year, my son—armed with the information he'd gleaned through his school project—decided he wanted to try being vegan for a week. My entire family joined him. Although I was apprehensive at first, I was surprised at how easy the transition was. Almost immediately, I felt my digestive system changing. I was eating veggies every day! No meat, no dairy, no animal by-products. The changes were so practical and we were feeling such immediate results that we decided to just keep on going and see what would happen. Weeks turned into months and months into years. I felt better than ever. I'd begun to shed weight, and my entire family became healthier.

The changes moved beyond the physical to the physiological. Now that I felt great, my mind and emotions transformed. Even my worship and faith began changing. I was shocked. Like my friend who had gone plant-based after surgery, I couldn't quite explain the hows and whys behind what was happening. All I knew was that by shifting my food intake, I was somehow becoming more in tune with the Spirit.

My purpose here is not to convince you to go vegan. It's to show you that there's a real connection between what you eat and how

> **There's a real connection between what you eat and how you feel.**

you feel. I was fueling my body in a way that was much more informed and intentional, and I could feel the change in every aspect of my life.

IT'S ALL CONNECTED

Health really is wealth—and it's also a big part of your agency. When you are operating at the peak level of health available to you, you're most capable of making your own choices, exercising freedom, and seeking total transformation. Consistent investment in your body increases your strength and energy, further equipping you to seek healing from mental and emotional trauma, face spiritual battles, and be increasingly present in your relationships. In other words, growth in the area of physical health is never an end in itself. It also exponentially increases your holistic health.

Without understanding the integrated nature of the mind, body, and spirit, however, you could be in danger of neglecting to care properly for the body our Creator gave you. He didn't make you just so you could experience life spiritually—he also made you with a body to experience physical life. Instead of viewing the body and spirit as separate spheres, you must recognize how the two are united.

Informed eating, regular exercise, and conscious care of your body aren't just about being "healthy." They are about self-care and good stewardship of the one body God gave you: "So, whether you eat or drink, or whatever you do, do all to the glory of God."[1] In this way, care for the body can be an act of worship.

THE DIVIDE

Eating is an act of faith, and caring for your body is a form of worship. Unfortunately, not everyone recognizes the unity of the body and the spirit. This leads to some seriously misinformed spiritual conditioning. Unknowingly, people who sincerely believe they're following the ways of Yeshua have actually been misled by the heresy of Gnosticism.

Gnosticism has been around since ancient times, and one of its basic teachings is that the physical world is evil. If the physical world is evil, then anything made of matter (including our bodies) is sinful. This belief is easily refuted. When our Creator made the world, he called everything he made "very good."[2] Nevertheless, Gnostic thinking persists, leading people to see evil as arising from the body and the physical world and creating the assumption that being spiritual means paying *less* attention to caring for your body. The Gnostic way declares that the body and the spirit are opposed to each other, and it demands that you choose one or the other. Gnosticism leads either to the abandonment of care for the physical body (mysticism) or to the abandonment of the spirit in pursuit of the mere physical (secularism). But the teachings of Yeshua unite body and spirit. This unity is made real in your life as you increasingly come to know God and know yourself.

Holistically caring for yourself and others removes significant barriers to seeking total transformation. I've seen this play out in my own life. As I mentioned earlier in this chapter, when I started eating clean and drinking water, my spiritual life grew. This is no coincidence.

When I changed my eating habits, my body, which is made in the image of my Creator and is the vehicle for my spiritual life, had more capacity because my soul was now resting in a healthy frame. As I've become more united in body and soul, my brain has begun operating differently and the Spirit has been engaging more of my life.

In the end, none of this is about simply losing weight or being healthy. By transforming my approach to my physical care, I'm facilitating holistic growth. I'm literally awakening a better me, and I want to help you awaken a better you.

INFORMED EATING

Awakening a better us means we must soberly assess how we relate to our bodies, beginning with how we nourish them. We must learn the right information to become informed about our food. This is especially true for those of us who grew up using food for surviving, not thriving.

When you're first starting out, it can feel tedious to learn the impact food has on the body, but not taking the time to do so can have steep consequences. According to a 2017 study by the Global Burden of Disease, one in five people die annually due to a poor diet.[3] After rigorously investigating the relationship between dietary habits and chronic noncommunicable diseases among adults in 195 countries, researchers have concluded that poor dietary habits contribute to eleven million avoidable deaths every year.[4] This statistic includes more than just people in destitute regions dying of starvation. Even if you've never gone hungry a day in your life, a diet short on veggies, seeds, and nuts but heavy on sugar, salt, and trans fats can still be the death of you—as it was of my dad.

My unhealthy eating habits were leading me down the same path my father had taken. I needed more than a trendy diet plan. I needed the right information about food and a transformed view of physical health. But seeking health transformation was not just about gathering information. I had to examine where I was getting my information and how it affected my relationship with food.

WE EAT WHAT WE KNOW

Most of us carry our childhood relationship with food into adult-hood. I grew up in a household that focused mainly on survival—having just enough to get by. This mindset informed my parents' approach to eating. They provided regular meals for me and my siblings so we never went hungry. Yet, looking back at the food we ate, I recognize that we had quantity but not quality. We ate mostly cheap foods that could be picked up at discount: ramen noodles, canned sardines, chips, artificial fruit juices, and lots of cheap lunch meat. These foods filled our bellies but didn't fill us with nutrients. Naturally, I began to equate *eating* with *feeling full*.

As I progressed into my young adult life, I still didn't think about my food choices in terms of nutrition. If any thought went into my decision-making at all, it was to ask what's cheap, what's fast, and what tastes good. I gravitated toward things like cheese-burgers and pizza.

Perhaps you can relate. If you also grew up on a survival-based diet, let me speak a word just for you. It's not your fault that you inherited habits of survival. It is your responsibility to learn the habits you need to thrive. Likewise, you should feel no shame if you unconsciously carried these generational habits into your adult life. This is an inheritance—if an unconsidered one.

Once you started buying your own food, you may have added items your parents never let you buy and cut out items you hated but were forced to eat. But for the most part, you probably kept your childhood habits. If your parents fed you sugary cereals with whole milk for breakfast, that's the morning routine you probably carried with you. If your parents regularly brought home a basket of fried chicken for dinner, you might now do the same. If you ate a lot of instant noodles and white rice growing up, those might be the first items you add to your cart now as an adult. If you grew up with almond milk, fresh fruit from the farmers market, and soy burgers, perhaps you brought those tastes with you into adulthood.

Take some time to consider what philosophy shaped your ingrained eating habits. Were you raised on a diet of convenience or a diet that valued wholesome nutrition? Either way, have you taken the time to study your diet for yourself? Or are you merely acting on the habits handed down to you culturally and generationally?

As you consider your daily food choices, ask yourself how many of them are conscious decisions based on knowledge and how many are subconscious actions based on habit. Have you ever taken the time to be sure you're basing your eating habits on reliable information? Where did your information come from, and is the source one you can trust? How much do you really know about the foods you consume on a regular basis? Where did they come from? What processes did they undergo before they landed on your plate? What ingredients are in them, and how do those ingredients interact with your body? What nutrients do you need daily, and do the foods you eat provide them?

Many of us arrive in adulthood having blindly accepted eating habits that are the result of conditioning rather than a conscious choice. As you uncover how your upbringing has affected your relationship with food, you are increasingly able to exercise your agency and make any necessary changes.

SELLING HEALTH

In altering our health habits and pressing toward transformation, we're unraveling the conditioning of our families of origin, our customs, and our cultures. It's also important to recognize how deeply we've been shaped by corporations and industries interested in selling us their products.

Market-driven economies are especially invested in shaping our thoughts about food and exercise, nudging us toward enlisting in their programs and consuming their products with little consideration for us as individuals. It's happening every day, all the time, perhaps without your awareness. Advertisements bombard you, both online and off, through pop-up ads, billboards, and TV commercials. Ads come on between YouTube clips, and commercials play over the radio on your Lyft driver's favorite station and slide between segments of your favorite podcasts. More insidiously, companies co-opt your friends and family to convert you to their brands via multilevel marketing schemes framed as social connection and entrepreneurship opportunities.

There's a lot that could be said about the commercialization of health and wellness, but for now let's discuss why we must be proactive about our health choices. Immersed as we are in a consumer-driven environment, we should be increasingly conscious not just of *what* we're buying (or buying into) but also *how* those products entered our radar and *why* we're convinced we need them.

Part of exercising agency is being able to consider something and measure its benefit. If you don't know what's in the food you're consuming, what benefits truly come from the health products you're relying on, or how the workout routines you're investing in are intended to benefit you, you have no way of intelligently evaluating them.

Perhaps your attitude toward your health up to this point has been something along the lines of, "If it ain't broke, don't fix it." Unfortunately, people with this mindset have the tendency to float along, never analyzing their choices until they're facing a sudden health crisis. Too many are running on youth and fumes. All it will take is one thing going wrong, and their lives could go completely off the rails.

If you assume you can be healthy without putting in any work or considering what you're consuming, your assumptions will eventually catch up with you—and by that point, you'll already be sick. Don't wait until your doctor tells you you're going to die to consider how you want to live.

PUSHING PAST LIMITATIONS

As we consider making changes to improve our wellness, I want to acknowledge that we are not all on equal footing here. Before we dive headfirst into this area, understand that we don't all approach eating habits and physical conditioning from the same angle.

Knowledge

When it comes to understanding food, we may land anywhere along the spectrum, from very informed to not so informed, based on how we were raised and the choices we've made since. While some people may need to make only a few tweaks to their current habits, others may need to unlearn and relearn an entirely new approach to food. At the outset, the process may feel completely overwhelming. Even after you've made some headway, you may find certain answers difficult to track down.

It's okay to take your time with this growth trajectory, and it's always wise to consult with professionals. Talk to your doctor about your own particular health risks when making major changes to your diet and consider consulting a nutritionist for pro tips.

Whatever you do, don't use an overwhelming lack of knowledge as an excuse to do nothing. Start small, act on what you learn, and move forward. Everyone starts somewhere, and if you're looking for a safe and encouraging environment, our coaches at Build a Better Us are here for you. We've helped thousands of people around the world reclaim their health without diet-related trauma, and we'd love to help you as well.

To get the ball rolling, I've included some questions at the end of this chapter to help you evaluate your starting point, but I recognize that not everyone is in a position to answer all of them. Due to your situation, you may know little to nothing about your culture, your generational habits, or your own medical history. This is not your fault. Just make the best decisions you can with the information at your disposal, and don't feel shame about things you can't control.

Budget

Your food budget is another factor that determines how you approach your journey toward food-informed eating. Most of us don't have bottomless pockets, and some may not be calling the shots when it comes to food purchases and household spending.

Further compounding the struggle, many communities in the United States are in food deserts where injustices keep healthy food away from inner-city areas. Even if we could have afforded it when I was growing up, my family would have had to drive thirty minutes for healthy food options, while affluent, mostly White, families had to drive just five minutes to reach those same choices.

Your current financial situation and location may require you to make choices that are different from those of other people. Although you may approach things differently, this is still a battle worth waging. We only have one of you, and we want you to be around for a long time.

Even if you can't afford to make big changes, small changes now could save you big down the road. A changed diet could lower your risk of osteoporosis, stroke, diabetes, heart attack, or cancer. Ask yourself, is your future well-being really where you want to be cutting corners? Investing in your health through nutritious foods can save you much more in the long run.

Even if you agree with that statement, you still might be wondering where the money to eat healthy will come from. After all, an eight-pack of ramen noodles and a pound of organic apples are quite different in price. If you're serious about your health, are there areas of your life where you're funneling funds that might be better spent on healthy choices? Are multiple streaming platforms of greater value to your household than your current life expectancy? Are manicured nails more important than a smoothly running digestive system? Must you own a closet full of shoes at the expense of the body those shoes carry around? Will your treat-yourself approach in the short term really help you in the long haul?

Making changes to our physical routines will always prove challenging, both because our current habits are so deeply ingrained and because there are often barriers of time and expense when getting started. Considering that physical health can support and enhance spiritual, mental, emotional, and relational health, there's no denying all the ways in which our lives could improve as a result of these changes.

Body

In addition to the limitations of our core knowledge and budgets, our bodies also have limits—some more than others. Given the wide array of hereditary diseases, genetic disorders, and developed conditions that can possibly affect us, I won't pretend that perfect health is attainable by everyone through sheer effort or will.

One of the reasons I don't outline a specific diet or exercise plan in this book is that we're all so different. It's important to remember this as you approach staying active and learning more about food. Above all else, you must know your own body and make decisions from an educated position. Remember, transformation is possible when our *desperation* drives us to seek the *right informa-tion* and proper *application.*

For me, a plant-based diet has been life-changing, but I've made modifications that suit my particular needs. (Currently, I'm what you might call "vegan-ish.") As you seek information, fight the temptation to get sucked into thinking that there's only one right application for everyone. Our bodies and needs are different. Just because an influencer hypes it doesn't mean it will work for you. You've got to be strategic.

- **Targeted Diets.** Here's where consulting a guide could prove to be key. When you do your own research about food-informed eating, various faddish diets always rise to the top. Don't just choose what is popular. Choose an approach to eating that's right for you and your body. Your choice might depend on a goal agreed upon by you and your doctor, the needs of your body at this phase of your life, or any number of factors. Slow down, consider your options, consult a doctor or nutritionist, and make a comprehen-sive plan. Create a food-informed approach that centers on your nutritional needs.
- **Allergies.** Allergies and sensitivities to certain foods sometimes manifest when you make new and broad changes to your diet. Allergies to foods such as nuts, dairy, shellfish, or gluten can really mess you up and derail your progress. If you suspect an allergy might be affecting you or if you're considering making changes to your existing diet and want to do so from the most informed position possible, talk to your general practitioner about running an allergy and sensitivity panel.
- **Individual Limits.** Each of our bodies has its own special quirks, meaning we have individual limits. We absolutely cannot all keep the same diets. Because my wife, Vanja, has low iron, a meatless diet isn't wise for her. That's okay. She doesn't have to eat the same

way I eat, and neither do you. We must know our own bodies and give them what they need. The principle of individual limits applies to exercise as well as diet. If you have physical limitations, it's likely you can still work out! Just don't feel the need to do what everyone else is doing. Check with your doctor, consult a trainer and/or physical therapist, and find a system that works with your physical realities.

As much as you will benefit from food-informed eating and regular physical activity, they aren't a cure-all, especially if you have a serious and irreversible condition. Only your Creator holds the power of life and death in his hands, and only he can ultimately heal you. What we can do is be good caretakers of the bodies we currently inhabit—limits and all. No matter your current situation, remember your reason for change. It will motivate you to move forward from where you are toward your optimal version of health.

KNOW YOUR "WHY"

I'm a Black man who follows a vegan diet. That shouldn't raise eyebrows, yet I find it often does. A lot of people associate the vegan lifestyle with rich, White millennials. Perhaps they view veganism as a faddish option for those who live on the 'Gram rather than a reasonable option for someone in pursuit of holistic health. In the Black community, healthy eaters are often seen as doing the most, seeking attention, being too picky. But that's not really the case. Health is for all of us, and we can all take part by overcoming resistance and getting ourselves on board. One thing that will fuel your determination is to know why you're committing to health.

Your reasons for pursuing health may be layered. Though a pursuit of health may outwardly demonstrate itself through changes to your physical appearance, those changes are only important in what they represent. You're not eating well and working out merely to change your appearance—body size doesn't determine health—but any potential changes to your appearance will represent changes on a cellular level, changes that will play out in your complete well-being.

This is where your "why" comes in. Maybe you want more energy to enjoy life with your community. Maybe you want to discover the version of yourself you've always suspected was possible. Perhaps your doctor has told you that you're at risk for serious health complications, or you're just tired of feeling bloated and listless. Maybe your eating habits and sedentary lifestyle have started to catch up with you, interfering with your quality of life. Maybe you want to live long enough to take your grandkids fishing. Perhaps you simply want to take better care of the one and only body your Creator gave you.

Whatever your reasons may be, knowing your "why" will bolster your determination, both to start the process and to see it through.

> **Knowing your "why" will bolster your determination, both to start the process and to see it through.**

When you have a solid understanding of your reason for change, you won't shy away from the struggles. Instead, you will confront the hard moments with confidence and propel yourself further toward awakening a better you.

FROM HARD TO HABIT

Yes, change is hard—but that's mostly in the beginning. As you grow in knowledge, change your intake one bite at a time, and develop a fitness routine, it will become less hard and more of a habit.

I'd felt inspired when I saw the food presentation at my son's school, but when I first started adjusting my diet, the process felt daunting—if not impossible. But as I sit here now considering all the benefits I've derived from pursuing health, I know I couldn't do without my new lifestyle, not to mention all the positive, tangible side effects of this journey.

I'd believed certain aspects of my health were unpreventable. But since I changed my diet, I've experienced a dramatic reversal with three specific issues that had plagued my adult life. Instead of riding the roller coaster of weight fluctuations, I've maintained a consistent appearance while feeling great. Rather than being frequently sick with colds, flus, and stomach bugs, I am healthier than I've ever been. And, as it turns out, my allergies hadn't merely been triggered by elements in my environment. They'd been affected by my diet. Since adopting a mostly plant-based diet, I've noticed my allergy symptoms have disappeared.

I had wrongly assumed that my weight, susceptibility to sickness, and allergies were all hereditary. I didn't realize what food was doing to me until I consulted an expert and acquired an informed view of what I was eating and how it was affecting me. I'd never suspected that the side effects I'd inherited from my family were passed down not only through genetics but also through habits. My grandparents raised my parents to raise me to eat a certain way. Then I made those generational habits my own. If I hadn't changed, I'd still be right there, subsisting on hot Cheetos, Takis, and Jungle Juice. But moving from unconscious habits to an intentional, informed approach changed my relationship with food—and with it, my life.

This is my hope for you: that you experience a similar transformation. That you move past uninformed consumption to conscious, informed food choices that work with, not against, your individual body. That your increasing physical wellness fuels your holistic health, energizing you to awaken a better you, one that encompasses all of who you are—mind, body, and spirit.

TALK IT OUT

1. How do cultures, communities, families of origin, and geographical locations play into our approach to physical health?
2. What are some common excuses people make for not seeking optimum physical health through diet and exercise? To what extent are these excuses based on lies? To what extent are they based on truth?

WORK IT OUT

List five words that currently describe your physical health:

Circle the term that best describes your current approach to food consumption:

- conventional
- vegetarian
- vegan
- pescatarian
- other: _____

In what ways is your current health plan working?

In what ways is it not working?

List the ways in which these three factors have informed your approach to food:

Culture

Generational Habits

Medical History

Read the following list and check the statements that are true of you:

- ☐ When I have questions about my approach to food and physical activity, I know whom to ask.
- ☐ I know where my food comes from.
- ☐ I know the processes my food has undergone before it reaches my plate.
- ☐ Generally, I know what ingredients are in my food.
- ☐ I know what nutrients I need daily and what foods I should eat to obtain them.
- ☐ I base my eating habits on reliable information.
- ☐ I have a fitness plan in place that takes into consideration my physical abilities and matches my health goals.

For the items you could not check, list specific steps you will take to seek answers:

WRITE IT OUT

Spend five minutes freewriting about your physical health: where you are right now, where you'd like to be, and why making changes matters to you.

7

Awaken a Better Relational You

I was excited to go to college, but my freshman year hit hard. I'd left Dallas and was new to my faith. I tried to keep in touch with some of my old friends, but none of my high school relationships were translating. I went from feeling loved and accepted and known by a community to having no one. I was isolated. Often, I would just sit in my little room listening to Christian music and reading the Bible by myself. It was hard to wake up like that, excited to be getting to know God but having no one to share this experience with. I needed connection with people who shared the same beliefs to help me grow. But where to begin?

What kind of relationships would the new me have? I knew I wanted friends with certain types of values—friends who lived righteously. But I didn't know where to find them or how to get started building those connections.

One day when I was at the gym, I saw this guy with a stocking cap on his head.

"I've seen you before," I told him, which was true. And I had questions. "What are you doing? What are you about? Who are you around?"

He stepped back and cocked his head to the side, clearly not sure what to make of me, my approach, and this sudden interrogation.

It wasn't the last time we would cross paths. The next time I saw him, we were at the same small group. I told him about this program I was putting together at a juvenile detention facility. I invited him to come with me the following week.

During the visit, my new friend performed music, then I got up to speak. It was the first time I had ever spoken in public, and it felt good that I wasn't there alone, trying to do it by myself. We seemed to work well, him and me. So, we kept on.

Two years later, he said to me, "When these kids get released, I want to send them home with an album." Fifteen tracks later, he had created something just for them. Then, in 2006, he released the album. Three years after that, the album went platinum.

The album was *Real Talk,* and the guy in the stocking cap was Lecrae.

Lecrae and I grew up together. We navigated our early days of faith and White evangelicalism together. It wasn't all good times. Like any friendship, we've experienced an ebb and flow involving disagreements, disillusionment, and depression. But our friendship doesn't shy away from the realities of life. It integrates them.

When Lecrae was interviewed on *The Breakfast Club* in 2020, he was asked how he kept the faith during a year that included a pandemic alongside racial, social, and political upheaval. Along with Scripture, music, meditation, and therapy, Lecrae credits close friends and "people around me who understand what I'm going through, who can look me in my face and not try to fix me but face me every day."[1]

Though we'd started as strangers, Lecrae and I grew together as friends. We worked together, collaborated, and built our skills together. And together, we launched a movement that would transform the spiritual lives of people around the world.

My friendship with Lecrae may sound unique, but it's actually not. This is how relationships are designed to work. In our friendships, family units, faith communities, and peer groups, this is what we can do for one another. We can form healthy bonds that allow us to navigate life's choppy waters. Over the long haul, we'll serve as both those who are guides and those who need guidance.

WE NEED ONE ANOTHER

God made us to be better together. We were created for relationships—to make meaningful connections and, through them, to share joy, sorrow, and the whole spectrum of human experience.

When the Creator made the first man and woman, he made them to reflect his image. As Father, Son, and Spirit, Yahweh will never experience lack. He does not need to look outside himself for anything, including relational connections. He needs no one's counsel but his own. Because we are in his image, we reflect his nature in our design, but because we are not fully sufficient in ourselves, we must look outside ourselves for relational fulfillment. That means we cannot experience the whole of our humanity alone. We need properly ordered relationships.

Your deep longing for meaningful connection is real and valid. That is why we ache so badly to be seen, known, heard, and loved. Without relationships with God and others, we will never truly feel whole. We need one another. When we have healthy relationships, we experience a depth of resources that will light the road to transformation.

But healthy relationships aren't intuitive. They're intentional, and that intentionality must be formed around mature practices and principles. Good relationships don't just happen. They must be built over time and wisely developed. If you fail to do that, you will either drift off into isolation or become entangled in dysfunctional dynamics. Neither is what your Creator intended.

Most of us don't need to be convinced of the importance of relationships. We know we wouldn't make it through life on our own. What we need is guidance in forming relationships, strengthening healthy bonds, and learning when to hold on and when to let go. All types of relationships go through natural phases of development. Phases that, when properly understood, can be consciously nurtured. Developing these areas can help you nurture healthy relationships that ultimately propel you toward awakening a better you.

PHASE ONE: BUILDING RELATIONSHIPS

Healthy relationships don't just happen, and they aren't accompanied by the perfect dialogues we find in movie scripts. What they do have is purpose. They're intentional. They are hard yet rewarding. They also have a mode of operation, one based on a deliberate commitment. Commitment establishes boundaries, boundaries create a safe space to build trust, and trust leads to intimacy.

Make a Commitment

The cornerstone of any relationship is commitment—a verbalized, mutual agreement to be both *with* each other and *for* each other. Once you've decided to commit to a relationship, that commitment must be verbally communicated. To place trust in someone when there is no verbalized commitment (or only an assumed commitment) is to run the risk of vulnerability with someone who is unwilling to back you up or who is unworthy of your trust. Without a firmly established commitment, deep relational investment can result in tremendous pain.

A UNIQUE BOND

Some believe that family relationships are the one type of connection in which there's a natural sense of trust without explicit agreements. However, it's possible to have a biological connection with no intimacy. Many of us have experienced that particular pain. Though many of us take the concept of family support and intimacy for granted, these bonds are forged and strengthened by our ongoing verbal commitments to be with one another and for one another.

This principle is generally best understood within the context of romantic attachments. When I was dating my wife, we had a DTR (defining the relationship) talk. Defining the relationship can be exciting or awkward depending on the response. Basically, it's asking, "Are we a couple or nah?" It's just as important to have a DTR talk for other types of relationships as well, from mentorships to friendships and everything in between.

It can feel awkward to verbalize a commitment if you've never done it before, but constructing a framework for intentionally investing in relationships doesn't have to be fancy or overblown (no need for champagne, matching tattoos, or secret handshakes). The process might look different depending on the people involved and the type of relationship being established, but defining the relationship is worth your time and energy.

Let me caution you: This isn't something that happens very often. You don't want to go around turning every new relational connection into an awkward conversation about someone's intentions. Verbalizing your commitment to a friendship—having a friendship DTR talk, if you will—is an informal process.

There's not necessarily a script to follow or a set of vows to be exchanged. (Can you imagine?) What we're talking about here is an acknowledgment that you and a friend who share the same values have recognized that you're moving forward together. By this point, you've spent enough time together that it's clear both parties are benefiting from the relationship. However you choose to say it, what you're really trying to verbalize is that your interactions have been so good so often that you want to establish a sense of commitment and intentionality.

At this level, it's always best to start small. "Do you want to get coffee together regularly?" Ask the question and wait to see how the other person responds. Check to see if they match your energy and demonstrate reciprocity. If they say, "Let's meet for an hour once a month," then you know they're also committing to the relationship.

A sure way to crush a friendship, however, is to put too much pressure on the relationship too soon or to ask for too much too fast. Instead, take small steps. Allow the level of your relationship to evolve naturally, always considering whether the other person responds in kind. This is important, because if you're the only one making the commitments and investments, then you might be assuming the other person feels something greater than they do. If you have to force it, it's not a mutual relationship.

When it comes to relationships, nothing should be taken for granted—at least not until you've already developed deep intimacy, and such intimacy can only develop through building trust in a committed relationship.

Establish Trust

Trust is the response to telling the truth and being known, and it's formed the old-fashioned way—over time. Only through spending time with each other, observing behavior and communicating on a deep level, are we able to trust deeply enough to share what we really think and let others see who we truly are. That doesn't mean the other party is accepting of all our ideas, but it does mean they're willing to accept the sum total of who we are, divergent opinions, whack fashion sense, and all.

This trust-building stage requires vulnerability, which is inherently risky. Fortunately, our pre-established commitment to be not just *with* one another but also *for* one another provides the confidence to open up. Through making commitments, establishing trust, and being vulnerable with one another, we create a safe environment where intimacy can flourish.

Since *vulnerability* is a bit of a buzzword right now, allow me to add a word of caution. Because vulnerability is so powerful, people often try to begin with vulnerability before even commitment, thinking its power will be sufficient to draw people in and keep them close. But if you lead with vulnerability, before establishing a mutual agreement to be *with* and *for* one another, you're exposing your most sensitive self in a fluid, undefined—and ultimately unsafe—relationship.

Only people who have both expressed care for you *and* demonstrated themselves committed to your well-being are worthy of your trust and deserve your vulnerability. Without that, they have not proven themselves willing, safe, or worthy of you.

Foster Intimacy

Our society tends to use the word *intimacy* exclusively in connection with sex. True intimacy, however, is not limited to romantic partners—it is the warm, familiar comfort of safe interdependence that's made possible within the context of a trust-filled relationship. Though some intimate relationships do indeed include sex, sex is not necessary for true intimacy. (Incidentally, there's plenty of evidence to suggest that intimacy leads to more fulfilling sex rather than the other way around.[2] Married readers, take note.)

We see evidence of this broader understanding of intimacy in the origins of human history. In Eden, Adam and Eve walked with God in complete intimacy. They knew their Creator personally, communed with him directly, and understood that he could see everything about them. This vulnerability never bothered them until shame entered the equation. After disobeying God's command by eating from the Tree of the Knowledge of Good and Evil, rather than maintaining vulnerability by coming to God right away, they tried to hide their disgrace with fig leaves.

As they soon discovered, covering their shame didn't help. Hiding shame cannot erase it, and in a truly intimate relationship, all is seen and known. Fortunately, God created a way through the shame by coming to Adam and Eve and sacrificing on their behalf. First, he clothed them with animal skins. Later, he would cover their shame with his glory through the person and work of Yeshua.

Humanity is a mess. You're a mess, and I'm a mess—but we're God's mess, and he deeply loves us. Just like the Creator came to find the couple in the garden, he has come to find us. Even in our worst moments, God's got us. He sees our mess and loves us anyway. This is the essence of intimacy, and we must strive to reflect this in the way we intentionally pursue our relationships with others.

We can't do work within our relationships exactly like God does, but his actions model a process to follow. True intimacy does not hinge on perfection, and it cannot exist when we attempt to hide our shame from one another. In most cases, we can't hide it, anyway; if we try, we have to hide the realest and most genuine parts of ourselves.

True intimacy comes about when we are able to come to someone directly and be seen for who we really are, with our unique blend of strength and human brokenness. Intimate relationships are the ones in which we can say to one another, "Yes, you are a mess—but you are my mess."

Intimacy means you know someone inside and out—the good and the bad—and you still keep dealing with them. The good doesn't make them more worthy, and the bad doesn't make them less. In truly intimate relationships, we get to be messes together. You know each other's thoughts, feelings, and opinions well enough to predict reactions. You can read each other's minds and finish each other's sentences. You can let down your guard and be yourselves. Though you still have to give of yourself, you no longer have to labor to maintain a facade or explain yourself. In an intimate relationship, you're free to just be, to learn and grow and transform—together.

> **Intimate relationships are the ones in which we can say to one another, "Yes, you are a mess—but you are my mess."**

Climbing the Spiral Staircase

In general, we should strive to build relationships in the order described above—first commitment, then trust, then intimacy. However, this process is not always strictly linear. More often, it is like a never-ending spiral staircase—causing you to turn, adjust, and keep shifting your focus the further you rise.

As your relationships progress, the level of your mutual commitment deepens to reflect the trust being built, which in turn determines the amount of vulnerability you can display. As intimacy grows, our foundations of trust and commitment settle more deeply, allowing for even closer bonds. Similar to climbing a spiral staircase, as you progress in your relationships the views along the way do not stay the same, and neither does your perspective. But though both keep changing, the end goal stays the same, and the further you rise, the more you can see.

It is good to intentionally build our relationships, but no foundation lasts forever without ongoing care and maintenance. Once relationships have been established, they must be consistently cared for and reinforced in order to stay strong.

PHASE TWO: STRENGTHENING RELATIONSHIPS

Though God made us capable of functioning individually, we only mature collectively. Contrary to what pop psychology and Disney songs might tell you, the tools you need to expand critical parts of yourself aren't found inside yourself. They're developed as you work to strengthen committed relationships with others. Much like with daily exercise regimens, the amount and quality of the work you invest in your relationships will determine the rewards they produce over time. The longer you run, the more calories you burn. The more squats you do, the stronger your quads. The more you invest in your relationships, the stronger they'll grow.

That's why even good relationships feel like work—and why we're willing to invest in them even though they're so exhausting. There are tools you acquire, social skills you develop, character traits you hone, and critical parts of your personality that form only through connection to others. You need people, and they need you. There are pieces of you that will only come out through your connection to a certain individual. Somehow, you're smarter when talking with your sister. Funnier when out with your best friend. Able to access more keen insights during discussions with your dad.

Of course, the reverse is also true. People with the poorest relationships are often those with the grossest personal imbalances and immaturities. Which comes first—the chicken or the egg—is irrelevant. The results are the same. Working on yourself improves your relationships, and working on your relationships improves you. Read that again. Only once you awaken a better you can we all become a better us.

Relational Workouts

Practically speaking, maturing through building relationships with others is not always easy, but it's a necessary process to reach transformation. The difference between relationships in which we aim for deeper connections and those that are more superficial is like the difference between a lump of coal and a diamond. Technically, coal and diamonds are both formed from the same material—carbon. But only one has been transformed into something of great value and beauty.

Diamonds begin as lumps of carbon. Over time, these black lumps are exposed to high temperatures and pressures. Just like carbon must be exposed to an extreme environment before it combusts into a diamond, we must wrestle with God and others to discover the true beauty and value in who the Creator made us to be.

There are five deeply uncomfortable ways that we can actively engage with others to uncover unseen parts of who we are and awaken a better us.

Risk
Relationships are inherently risky. Deep down, we all know this. To protect ourselves, we seek comfort in relationships that are "easy." But spending time with people who are content to accept the status quo will never challenge us or help us transform into better versions of ourselves. In order to reach transformation, we must build a community in which we encourage one another to get out of our comfort zones.

Wrestling

Though you're right to avoid toxicity and drama, understand that a complete lack of friction in a relationship could be a red flag. A true relationship includes push and pull, give and take. Other people challenge, inspire, and correct us. They give us the nudge we need to move past points of desperation, seek the right information, look for the right application, and move toward transformation. Through wrestling with ideas, opinions, and personalities different from our own, we're stretched, molded, and changed. Uncomfortable? Yes. Tiring? Sure. Necessary for transformation? Absolutely.

Truth-Telling

When our only goal is to maintain peace in our relationships, we avoid speaking hard truths so as not to rock the boat. But if we're going to make transformation possible for ourselves and others, we must find the courage to speak up, challenge, and offer a counterbalance when needed. We must also be willing to receive the same from others. Striving to maintain peace at any cost in your relationships will never create an environment in which your community can learn, change, grow, thrive, and transform.

Empathy

While sympathy is a feeling of pity or sorrow for the misfortunes of others, empathy is the ability to enter into another's experience and share in the associated feelings. Dynamic relationships involve more than just feeling "for" each other. We must feel "with" each other. This sort of connection requires time, attention, intimacy, and consistent physical presence.

Humility

Do we allow people to question and push back on our words, actions, and motives? Are we capable of receiving correction? Do we model the humility of our Savior, Yeshua, who took the role of a servant and washed feet?

Nothing on this list is comfortable. Yet each item is necessary. When we are willing to be humbly refined in the fires of a healthy relationship, to step out of our comfort zones and develop these traits, then we will experience the full beauty of our relationships—and open the door to transformation.

RELATIONAL PRACTICALITIES

If we're going to invest properly in our relationships, we must consider what goes into building and maintaining them day by day. It's fine to talk about these principles in theory, but what does creating and nurturing healthy relationships look like practically?

Make Time

Relationships grow through connection and intentionally spending time together. Only when you're currently investing personal time and attention in someone's life can you consider yourself in a relationship with that person. Without an intentional investment of time, what you have is static at best—on its way to the morgue at worst. No matter the nature of the relationship, intentionality is what will keep it alive. Relationships can only be sensibly said to exist when there is an ongoing investment of time, care, and energy.

Establish Boundaries

There's a desperate beauty at the ocean's edge. That's why so many people love driving California's Pacific Coast Highway and why so many dating profiles list "long walks on the beach" as an activity of choice. (At least, that's what I hear. I'm not on dating apps. Hashtag happily married.) What we love is not so much the ocean itself but the beauty we observe when we're in safe proximity to it. When observed from a blanket on the beach or through a thick pane of glass at the aquarium, marine life is mesmerizing. Out of its proper context, it's terrifying.

Consider the aftermath of Hurricane Harvey in 2017. After churning slowly through the Gulf of Mexico, Harvey made landfall. Currently on record as the wettest Atlantic hurricane ever measured, Harvey unleashed more than twenty-seven trillion gallons of rain on the state of Texas. One-third of Houston completely flooded. The massive storm surge and heavy rains damaged or destroyed one million cars and 135,000 homes. Experts estimate that it caused around $125 billion in damage. Worse still, the storm led to either the direct or indirect deaths of over one hundred people.[3]

The beach is beautiful, until it's in the middle of your living room. Same water, same sea life, same power, but without proper boundaries to keep you safe, the most beautiful thing in the world becomes the most destructive. Like shorelines protect us from the ocean, boundaries safeguard our relationships. Boundaries define parameters, holding potentially destructive forces in their proper place and creating a safe space in which we can encourage one another along the road to transformation.

Live in Reality

In order to build strong and healthy relationships, real-time, face-to-face meetings are best. Not to knock FaceTime, but certain things can only be accomplished through physical presence. While there may be seasons when technology has to get you through (when one of you is traveling, for instance, or we are experiencing a prolonged public health crisis), it cannot be relied upon to bear the weight of our most meaningful connections. The same can be said of email, text, phone calls, or any other form of communication that eliminates the need to meet in person.

Share Your Story

No one else has a story quite like yours. Whether it's your past, your faith journey, what you've overcome, or where you feel God's drawing you in the future, you have something unique to share. No matter who you are, your story is significant. Without even meeting you, I know this is true. Why? Because I know your Creator. He made everything with a purpose—and that includes you. Sharing your story can inspire others and encourage them in their own journeys toward transformation.

Break Bread Together

There is nothing like a family reunion, I would argue, especially a Black folks' "Cousin Pete" family reunion. Across cultures, gathering over food and drink is a strong, social-bonding experience. Taking time to share a meal, whether it's a feast or humble fare, promotes bonding, intimacy, and relational warmth. The description of the early church's social interactions, particularly allusions to an agape feast in the New Testament, point to an established tradition of saints gathering to break bread with one another.[4] Get your people together and eat some food. Share the gifts of fellowship and flavor.

PHASE THREE: NAVIGATING THE EBB AND FLOW OF RELATIONSHIPS

God created seasons—and I'm not just talking about summer, fall, winter, and spring. In the wisdom book of Ecclesiastes, Solomon reminds us that the Creator has ordained the seasonal pattern throughout all aspects of life: "For everything there is a season, and a time for every matter under heaven."[5]

If there's truly a season for everything, then there's a time for relationships to form and a time for them to end. An important factor in maintaining healthy relationships is learning to recognize when a relational connection has changed or is dead. We'll talk more in the next section about practical ways to know when to let go of a relationship and when to hold on. For now, know that relationships require intentional building and strengthening. They also require us to navigate the ebb and flow that naturally results when life changes. We find the best example of what this approach looks like by considering the life of Yeshua himself.

Yeshua and Relationships

If you study Yeshua's time on earth, you'll note that he did not, in fact, treat everyone in the same way. The nature of his interactions with the people around him, the kind of energy he brought to people, and the amount of time he invested differed. Because he is literally God and God is love, the way Yeshua treated people was always an outflow of that love. Remember that. Yeshua's ministry wasn't about reserving love and care for only some people. It was about knowing how to best express his love and care at different times and places to different people in different ways.

While Yeshua reserved harsh words for the proud and self-righteous religious elites, he offered gentle comfort to the broken and humble. Because he loved them all, he was giving each exactly what they needed to learn and grow. Similarly, he was unapologetic about how he invested his time—and with whom he spent it. Though he met countless people during his short time of active ministry, he invited only twelve into a special relationship as disciples. Of those twelve, only three were called into deeper intimacy, and only one was actually called "beloved" (John).

Yeshua understood that during his time as God incarnate, there was only so much time and energy that he could pour into relationships. He couldn't give the same level of attention to everyone he met—especially not to the crowds. To those not chosen as disciples, he gave some time and energy, but not all he had. Ultimately, when the crowds began to thin, their departure did not sway him from pursuing his ultimate purpose. Why? Although the masses would benefit from his acts of love, meeting their varying expectations was not his primary agenda. He focused relationally on a smaller group of people. Instead of getting sidetracked by those who made the most noise, he separated out those he intended to use and poured himself into them. The disciples were, essentially, what we would consider a small group. But look what resulted from his investment in them. By spreading his message through the power of the Spirit, the disciples changed the world.

Ultimately, making room to invest in different relationships in very specific ways is one of the most effective and loving things you can do—both for yourself and for your community. Not only does it keep you from stretching yourself too thin, but it also ensures that you are investing your time and energy in the best possible ways to help yourself and others transform.

Honestly, most of us won't be dealing with the types of crowds Jesus did. (Let the introverts say amen.) The dangers for most of us center more on not approaching different types of relationships with wisdom and forethought.

Making Room

Part of the reason we don't get the most out of our relationships is that we don't enter them with clear expectations. Outside of delineating family from friends, we don't have any divisions or categories in our minds. Because we don't have an established relational framework, we allow people to occupy outsize portions of our attention, crowding out the space real connections could fill. Categorizing relationships isn't about dividing our connections into some type of grid. It's about soberly processing the nature of our relationships and evaluating whether we're doing what we can to love and serve our people well, particularly over time.

Although we won't be delving too deeply into the nature of family dynamics in this book, it's important to note that the categories we're about to discuss apply only to people outside our family. For most of us, our family members are our primary emotional anchors. We did not choose these relationships for ourselves; our role is to maintain them as best we can. Though some connections require more maintenance than others, family members are likely to be in our lives for a long time, regardless. The relationships listed in the following pages are not a substitute for your family but a supplement to them.

Establishing healthy relationships throughout your evolving phases of life requires making room for others. This means you won't maintain all your relationships throughout your entire life—at least, not all at the same level. And that's okay. You actually need connections that grow and evolve as you do. Different types of relationships help bring out the multifaceted beauty of who you are. To that end, you don't just need a person—you need people. And making room for others to enter your life in a real way means doing the work necessary to keep space available. Most of the people in our lives will take on one of these five roles: mentors, mentees, peers, colleagues, and associates.

Mentors

The title *mentor* should not be applied loosely, and a sharp distinction should be made between mentors and role models. Role models are people we look to from a distance, admiring their successes and perhaps even striving to emulate them. Role models offer a finished picture for you to admire. Mentors sit down beside you, hand you a brush, and show you how to paint your own.

In that sense, mentors aren't just people you look up to or admire (though if you're considering someone as a mentor, you should admire them). True mentors are individuals who are ahead of you in the direction you're heading; they must also have agreed to mentor you. Both aspects are critical. No one can take you down a path they haven't already walked themselves, and without a clearly defined relationship, the mentoring role does not exist.

Mentors carry on personal relationships with you in partnerships intended to amplify your strengths and reduce your weaknesses. Mentors don't just give you an example to follow; they intentionally commit to walking with you, critiquing your efforts and holding you accountable. Their words carry great authority in your life because they're already "in it"—living the thing you're still aspiring to accomplish. Mentors are given a level of access and influence in your life that role models could never touch because your mentor knows you, cares about you, and is personally invested in your success.

Here's an important flip side to consider: Whatever is true of your mentors is also equally *not* true of people who are *not* your mentors. Not just anyone has the right to speak authoritatively into your life, and not everyone should be invited to do so. While there will always be folks offering free advice, you are always free to not take it. The targeted wisdom of our chosen mentors deserves an elevated status that the "wisdom" of opinionated bystanders can never touch.

Though mentorship relationships are valuable, they are still ultimately seasonal. It can be hard to change gears sometimes, but

you must acknowledge that even
your most respected mentors will
not stay your mentors forever. Ultimately, that's a good thing. It
means you've grown, changed,
and moved one step closer to
transformation! Although you
won't cut beloved mentors out of
your life once they've developed
you as far as their knowledge has

> **Not just anyone has the right to speak authoritatively into your life, and not everyone should be invited to do so.**

permitted, you must prepare to recognize when a season of mentorship has passed and know how to transition into a peer relationship without causing damage.

Mentees

Being able to mentor someone coming along behind us is both a
blessing and a challenge. Mentees don't just need us. We also need
them. Mentees remind us of where we came from and of basic
truths we're all too eager to forget—lessons we learned during our
own periods of struggle, failure, and discouragement. As we talk
mentees through long stretches of labor and self-doubt, we're re-
minded of how hopeless we felt when we were sitting where they
are now and how much help we have received along the way.
Without these reminders, it would be easy to look back on our
lives and careers through rose-tinted glasses, allowing our personal
pride to smooth the rough patches and cover over every blemish.

Our ultimate goal in mentoring others, of course, is to promote
flourishing to the point that our mentees become our peers. When
it comes to transitioning these relationships, acknowledging that a
mentee has outgrown you is both a joyful moment (this is what
you've been working toward!) and also a possible blow to your

pride (they don't need you anymore!). The process is much easier to navigate if you build the expectation directly into the relationship. It's hard to know exactly when your mentee needs to move on, but if they are the one hinting that the time has come, you've probably already waited too long.

Peers

I grew up with adults referring to everyone around my age as my "peers." At some point, though, we all outgrew that definition. Your peers are those in your life who refine and inspire you, whose interactions spur you on. Though they're not mentors, they still offer course corrections, and they will receive the same from you, though they are not your mentees. Instead of walking ahead of you or behind you, your peers move beside you on the road to transformation, right in the thick of things.

Peers don't necessarily need to be near you in age or have the same pursuits. Your peers are those people woven throughout your life who make the fabric tighter and stronger through their presence. In peer relationships, you can be heard, seen, known, and loved in a way that is not exhausting to maintain. Your companionship is a natural outflow of who you both are. When you encourage this sort of mindset in one another, you both become stronger.

While we may always maintain an ongoing sense of affection for those who have been our peers at different times, recognizing who your peers are at the moment and knowing how to judge when a peer relationship has come to an end are absolutely vital skills. Staying too long in a peer relationship (or considering someone a peer who is not actually one) can lead to disordered relationship structures and misappropriated time and attention. These relationships can consume a lot of your time and attention without doing you or the other person much good. Reordering these relationships doesn't mean that we cut these people out of our lives, but we discover the true nature of our relationship and approach it accordingly.

Colleagues

On the surface, the colleague relationship may look like many others on this list, but at the root, it's more conditional. Colleagues co-exist in labor, sharing information and responsibilities as needed. They may also share a sense of affection or friendliness, but their interactions are based more on workflow than on intimacy. While shared work experience may create a situational approximation of a bond, these connections rarely last past the job that brought you together in the first place. When that happens, it doesn't necessarily mean you failed relationally. On the contrary. Trying to carry all these relationships with you when you step away from a place of employment can prove a needless burden in the long run.

It's not that we don't love our colleagues. It's not that we don't value the place they've held in our lives, our experiences, and our memories. In fact, working with them has likely made us better people! It's just that we don't need to force these connections beyond their natural life cycle.

Associates

An associate is anyone who does not fit naturally into any of the four categories listed previously, yet is a consistent presence in our lives. Despite their consistency and proximity, associates are people with whom you maintain only surface interactions. Most people you meet will stay forever in this category—and that's okay. Some will move into other roles as you get to know them and/or as you both grow and change through seasons of life. Some people who once took more important roles in your life may move back to becoming associates over time.

Learning to see people as associates doesn't mean that you see them as less valuable or that you are mentally giving them a demotion. It just means that as the story of your life develops, you become more conscious of yourself as a main character and of where others stand in relation to the grander scheme of your main story line.

WRITING OUR STORIES

Writing this book has been so eye-opening. Before this experience, I thought authors just sat down, put their thoughts on the page, and sent them off to the publisher, ready to be made into books. Nobody told me anything about drafts. About writing multiple versions of the same chapter until I got it right. About letting people read early versions and letting them have some say about what's working, what's not working, and what might need to be cut. About how editors would get involved.

One thing I've learned is that no writer is above a good editor. Even Stephen King has editors. (Probably.) Editors review your work with unbiased eyes and offer expert advice on your manuscript. Just as no book is above editing, so no relationship is above evaluating. Nobody gets a pass. If relating this idea to relationships already has you panicking, keep reading.

The goal in evaluating relationships is not to cut them unnecessarily but to revise them based on their places in the overall story arc. Good storytellers have a knack for this. They know that when stories try to pack in too much and spiral out of control, nobody wants to read them. When the stories are cut down and honed to perfection, though, they're a smash hit. Just like writers do, you may have to cut some characters and revise other roles until your relationships are lean and focused. The next thing you know, your transformation becomes your own personal bestseller.

That's why a large factor in awakening a better us through healthy relationships is learning to recognize when a character or relational connection needs to be revised or cut. This step is not easy, but it is necessary. If you avoid it, you'll linger in spaces and connections for much longer than you should and hinder your progress toward transformation, like I did when I went to college.

How the Story Goes

Since childhood, I have always formed small but very tight friend groups with people from either my school or neighborhood. I would spend all my time with virtually one set—a group of friends from the hood like me. Our relationships were based on mutual respect, a shared upbringing, and the fact we were all prepared to fight for one another. We were inseparable—or so I thought.

In college, I began to grow exponentially; however, I hadn't soberly considered how the transition might affect my childhood friendships. I'd undergone massive inner shifts, but I did not allow them to be reflected honestly in my relationships. There were pieces of myself I'd downplay whenever my friends and I were together, just to keep the peace and try to get along. This was exhausting to maintain over time, and my developing character, faith, and life trajectory virtually ensured either a breakup or a breakdown.

Eventually it all came to a head when one of my closest friends and I got into a huge verbal altercation, one that neither of us could really explain. At the time, our fight seemed to bubble up out of nowhere, but the conflict had been brewing for a while. In the past, he and I had moved forward in sync as brothers, but now our conversations led to mutual frustration rather than flourishing.

It's not that I didn't love or care about this friend anymore. I saw him as my brother. But due to the different directions we'd taken in life, spending time together now drained me rather than enriched me. He probably felt the same way. If so, I wouldn't know. I wasn't mature enough to tackle that sort of conversation. Instead, we fruitlessly poured energy into a connection that could no longer bear intellectual, emotional, or spiritual weight.

You can't undo the chapters of life already written, but you can refine your focus as you move forward. To do so, ask for discernment to know which relationships should carry over into your next chapter, which ones should be revised, and which ones should be cut. Sit down with the five relationship categories listed previously—mentors, mentees, peers, colleagues, and associates—and take time to soberly process two things: (1) where your relationships currently stand and (2) how you should interact in each case moving forward.

Remember, revising your approach in relationships is not a judgment on anyone's value or worth. It's a simple recognition that someone's role in your life (or yours in theirs) has shifted, and to honor that shift, you are going to behave differently moving forward.

Cutting Characters

While most relationships simply need to be revised, a few should be cut entirely. People who are legitimately harmful, having consistently proven themselves to be liars, toxic, or abusive, should not come with you into your next chapter.

I want to caution you to apply those labels with care. Everyone who bothers you is not toxic. Part of God's method for refining us is to put us in relationships that require us to exercise mercy, patience, and grace. We are to bear with one another in love, overlook grievances, and be patient with one another.

While not everyone who gives you grief can or should be cut

out of your life, genuinely harmful people must be soberly considered. People who have abused you, demonstrated a clear and unrepentant pattern of lying, or consistently demoralized you through belittling speech and behaviors should be carefully evaluated. Cutting such people out of your life may feel impossible in the moment, but it will ultimately free you to seek transformation.

Cutting is rare, though. In most cases, you simply need to reorder relationships so that you can move forward, so that the people in your current chapter can get the most out of you and everyone connected can flourish. A few simple considerations can take much of the stress out of making these evaluations.

EVALUATING THE CHARACTERS

Evaluating the characters in your current chapter is as easy as looking at your communication stats. Check out your call logs from this week. Flip through your text history. Skim through Messenger. Make a list of who you spent time with face-to-face in the last ten days.

Write down the names of all these people and ask yourself if they represent purpose-filled relationships worthy of investing your time and attention. Are these people part of what's going on with you right now? Are they aware of your big picture? Are they reminding you of important truths that you need to know? Are they refining and inspiring you in this season? Are they giving you critical information or helping hone your skills? If not, they don't need to go into the next chapter with you. They'll still be part of your book of life, but they don't need to dominate the current story arc.

In books, we don't expect every character to appear in every chapter, and neither should we in real life. Sometimes people fall behind as the pages turn; sometimes their roles just change. New chapters often bring in fresh faces, and we need to leave room for them in the story. If you're seeking transformation, it won't be possible to bring every single person from your life along with you. They have their own stories to tell. How do you evaluate and reorder your relationships so you and everyone in your life make progress over the long haul, though?

Consider Your Story Goals

Writers develop characters based on books' overall story goals. As the authors develop the story lines, they will decide which characters need to appear in which scenes in order for events to fall in place. We can use a similar framework to evaluate our relationships.

Do we have goals for our relationships within the overall story of our lives? Do we know what we even expect from our relationships? In general, the needs within our relationships mirror the basic four human desires that we all share: to be heard, to be seen, to be known, and to belong.

Being able to satisfy those needs for others, while simultaneously having them fulfilled in our own relationships, is the essence of awakening a better relational you. By evaluating your story and the roles of the people joining you along the journey, you can move from a state of relational desperation to community transformation.

GO TO WORK

Relationships take work and time, but there are pieces of you that will only be developed through connections that move you toward your purpose. Until you are willing to take stock and work to reorder your relationships, you will continue to feel tired and stuck, losing all your energy to dead relationships rather than fostering ones fit to revitalize your current season. You will deflate rather than transform.

As you saw in the story about my childhood friend, I didn't always know how to adjust my relationships. In my immaturity at the time, I walked away from that friendship without saying anything. While it was clearly time for a change, the way I approached it was abrupt and hurtful. Call me Casper the Ghost.

Knowing what I do now, when I realize a relationship is nearing the end of its life cycle, I don't just abruptly ghost. Instead, I acknowledge what's happening and make a mental and emotional pivot. As a result, moving forward, I give less of myself to the person than I had up to that point, while making room for the people who will move with me into my future. With a bit of care and attention, I can transition the nature of our connection so that it's not traumatizing for either of us. We can both move forward in a new, healthier way.

Healthy relationships are like healthy bodies—they don't just happen. Health takes effort, and this effort takes three specific shapes: time, energy, and emotional work. It's a potentially scary process; I won't sugarcoat that.

Sometimes it's painful

- to realize that a chapter is closing
- to acknowledge that someone you considered a mentor isn't a mentor anymore
- to admit that you've outgrown people you've always considered peers

These are no small matters, but when you have the courage to face them, you're able to make space in your life for relationships that should actually be there. Together, you and the people in your life can help each other awaken better versions of yourselves, spurring one another on toward mutual transformation.

TALK IT OUT

1. How might disordered relationships hinder us from pursuing transformation?
2. Completely cutting people out of our lives should be rare. Under what circumstances should that happen? What is so difficult about making those cuts even when we know they're necessary? With what attitude should we approach this process?
3. How can we as a community encourage one another to order our relationships well?

WORK IT OUT

Just like an actual ship, your relationships should have both purpose and direction. In other words, all relationships are taking you somewhere on the ocean of life. Are you giving energy to the ones that fuel your purpose?

Consider the three most important relationships in your life. Use the following space to articulate the purpose and direction of each.

Relationship 1: _____

Purpose:

Direction:

Relationship 2: _____

Purpose:

Direction:

Relationship 3: _____

Purpose:

Direction:

After considering the relationship categories detailed in this chapter, take some time to consider your current connections. Who should be in the following categories and why?

Mentors

Mentees

Peers

Colleagues

Associates

Do you currently have a mentor? If so, who is it? If not, who would you choose to be a mentor?

What is your mentor doing to help you with your big picture in this season? (If you don't have a mentor, then use this space to imagine how a mentor could support you during this season.)

Do you have any mentees? Why or why not?

What are you doing specifically to help them move toward their purpose?

Do your peers refine and inspire you in your current season? Are you doing the same things for them? If so, list specific examples.

Think of times when you've allowed relationships with colleagues and associates to overshadow more vital relationships. What steps will you take to ensure this will not happen again?

WRITE IT OUT

Spend five minutes freewriting about relational intimacy. How might evaluating your relationships and intentionally naming and ordering them help propel you toward transformation?

8

Awaken a Better Spiritual You

In the fall of 2016, the state of American politics felt truly unhinged. It was an election year, and the final nominations for the major political parties had boiled down to Donald Trump and Hillary Clinton. It felt as if, rather than soberly processing the pros and cons of each candidate, the vast majority of Christians around me were fully invested in fighting a culture war, voting so that "our side" won, no matter the cost. And clearly, there would be a cost, if only to our Christian reputation. Already, there had been so many outlandish moments that I felt surely there was no way this reality-TV star could win the presidency.

I'd come to faith during college, and since that time, I'd been living in a sacred bubble. There, I learned that within my new Christian subculture, people's votes were seen as reflections of their faith. Yet despite lip service to Christian values, during this most recent election cycle, evangelical voters had largely thrown their allegiance behind Trump. Here was a man who had openly admitted to sexual assault, who had multiple baby mommas, had mocked disabled people, and had said so many crass and vulgar things that I'd already lost track. Was he really being held up as a reflection of our faith? Anytime a new story broke about something horrible he'd said or done, my inner Killmonger threw up his hands in a gesture of frustrated defiance: "Is *this* your king?"[1]

That a people who held "love thy neighbour as thyself" as a central tenet would support—and even seemingly *enjoy*—someone of such caliber was astounding.[2] The cognitive dissonance was on another level. Such support should have been completely unbecoming to a person of faith. Yet here we were repeating the mistakes of Israel who wanted a king like the other nations had—one void of God's standard though using God's words.

The night of the presidential election in November 2016, I was in Colorado at an event with a group of conservative (mostly White) Christians. When Trump's win was announced, I was devastated. It had actually happened. The next morning, I could hardly get out of bed. I needed to make an appearance at the conference, but my arms and legs refused to cooperate. They could barely propel me through my morning routine. Somehow, I dragged myself from my room and headed to the first session.

There, I entered another world—a world in which nothing had gone wrong. I encountered bright eyes, smiling faces. I witnessed no weeping, no mourning. There was seemingly no awareness of what this vote meant to women, those with disabilities, the marginalized, the Black community, and other ethnic minorities. There was no evidence of concern whatsoever. As far as I could tell, for the majority of my fellow attendees, this was just another morning after just another election.

I was shook.

Since Yeshua had redeemed me during my college days, my life had been formed around serving him. I'd helped launch 116, a massive Christian movement, and had been zealous for him in a way that had impacted the entire world. Now I found myself wondering how this "Christianity" stuff even worked. Was any of this about loving and serving people like Yeshua had—or had it all been just about winning a culture war? I'd thought I had a firm grip on life, my faith, my community, and how it all fit together. Now I was left reeling. Had it all been an act?

My faith went into a skid, and my life in my subculture crashed and burned. Relationships fractured. Lines were being drawn in the sand. I was pretty sure I was still a Christian, but American evangelicalism could no longer be my spiritual home. It felt like the end of everything. But through it all, I was to learn a crucial spiritual lesson: There's life outside the bubble.

LIFE BEYOND THE BUBBLE

After the 2016 election, I embarked on a painful journey that lasted over a year and a half. During this time, I couldn't read certain sections of the Bible. I could no longer reconcile what Scripture explicitly taught with the practices of people of faith I'd formerly admired. The mental gymnastics required were simply too demanding. I started struggling to pray, fearing God might not be who I thought he was—what if he turned out to be like them too?

I needed help, yet within my circles, no one seemed equipped to address this need. Anytime I came near broaching the subject, all I received back was invalidation, venting, or deflecting. I was told I was doing too much—being extra—overreacting. That I was "sensitive." From where I stood, there were no voices to follow on this, no leadership to pursue. No tools in my tool kit could help with a work of this magnitude.

I was stuck, trapped in a spiritual system with no solutions for my turmoil. As heartbreaking as this realization was, there was also hope. My Creator shined his light into the darkness. He showed me something about himself I'd never seen before.

God is infinite, which means he can't be contained by anyone or anything. No matter how far off track any of his followers stray, his true essence cannot be diminished. He doesn't fit neatly into any one system, including the evangelical bubble I'd lived in for so long. Yes, he had been there beside me. But he also lived outside the bubble. If he was present and powerful everywhere, then no matter where I went, if he was already there, I could survive.

Despite having believed for quite some time that there was no life beyond the bubble, I now recognized that if help were ever to reach me, it might have to come from somewhere out there. Still, I hesitated. Could I operate outside my sacred institutions and still retain genuine faith? If so, how?

With these questions, I took the first steps in a true walk of faith. Though new and uncomfortable to me, it was the same path the saints have trodden down through the ages. This was a call to the wilderness, and as I was to learn, this call was an invitation, not a devastation. If we know how to look, we can recognize this same journey in the lives of Old Testament prophets such as Moses and in the person and work of Yeshua himself.

This was a call to the wilderness, and as I was to learn, this call was an invitation, not a devastation.

IN THE WILDERNESS

Throughout Scripture, the wilderness is often the backdrop for transformative experiences. Many times, God brought people into the wilderness—the literal wilderness—in order to work in and through them. In the wilderness, Hagar sought Yahweh's intervention after being thrown out by Sarah. Elijah heard the still, small voice of God. John the Baptist prophesied. Yeshua faced temptation. Desperate circumstances drove them out from places of seeming comfort and security, and in the wilderness, they saw their faith transform.

Of all the people in Scripture, perhaps Moses had the longest and most intense experience with the wilderness. Moses hadn't grown up in a spiritual bubble. Quite the opposite. Due to circumstances beyond his control, Moses was raised in spiritual, cultural, and institutional structures foreign to his family of origin. Though born into a humble Hebrew household, he'd come of age in the courts of an Egyptian pharaoh. When Moses's life was threatened in infancy, God allowed the pharaoh's daughter to adopt him, and he was raised a son of the kingdom, with full rights and privileges. Yet despite the fact that God placed Moses in a position of apparent power, he began working uniquely through Moses only after he'd fled the royal courts into the Egyptian wilderness.

We don't know a lot about how Moses felt when he left Egypt. Did it feel like an abandonment? Did he feel lost, cast aside, forgotten? And yet in the wilderness, Moses truly experienced the power and presence of his God. In a place of arid wind, blistering sun, low population density, and extreme temperatures. A place with few resources, structures, and systems. Despite everything the wilderness lacked, it was there Moses found everything he needed. There, God refined and restored his faith. And in the wilderness, God would do the same for the Israelites.

Moses went back to Egypt and led the Israelites through the miraculously parted Red Sea and into the desert. While enslaved in Egypt, though, the Israelites had become accustomed to a certain way of life. It wasn't ideal, but it was what they knew—foods, comfort levels, and modes of living. After the initial euphoria of escape faded, they actually began to miss Egypt. They felt the withdrawal so keenly that, at one point, they expressed regret that they were no longer enslaved![3]

In the wilderness, the Israelites unlearned the ways of their oppressors. The forty years they spent wandering before entering the Promised Land gave them space to reconstruct their faith. To learn accurate information about the God they served. To find out what it meant to rely on God and God alone. Those who eventually entered the Promised Land had developed a mature faith while applying the lessons they learned in the wilderness. They were prepared to face the giants, armies, and terrors in the land. Their faith had been transformed.

DANGERS AND NEW LIFE

You, too, may be feeling the pull of the wild—a desire to deconstruct your faith, to wrestle with the inconsistencies and injustices—but life in the wilderness feels wild and uncontrolled. The rain and wind come and go with unpredictable strength and frequency. The sun follows its own schedule. Plants are scattered, bunched in messy clusters. In that sense, the wilderness can seem dangerous and terrifying. Though it seems chaotic at first, there's a method in the madness. There is a Divine Controller of all things. He is there, and nothing is ever beyond the reach of his hands.

Stepping into the wilderness may sound scary, but like those who came before us in the faith, we can heed the call to unlearn and relearn, to transform our faith as it is refined by new wilderness experiences.

Of course, there are dangers to the wilderness. People who have spent a long time sheltered from the elements may have a weakened spiritual immune system and anemic faith. The fear of unknown dangers and obstacles is a significant barrier. Those who have never traversed outside their spiritual bubble aren't sure what to expect or what their faith will look like outside their current context. Given the dangers at hand, they wonder if it's worth it—they could lose their way in the wild. Those who have never left their spiritual bubble will likely experience disorientation when they leave their current context. But the only way to really move beyond the bubble is to be willing to risk comforts for the sake of confidence. Yes, in the wilderness, there is darkness. But there is also light. God is not absent in the wilderness—indeed, he is not absent anywhere. In the wilderness, we transform our faith when we learn to rely on God's sufficiency.

HIS GRACE IS SUFFICIENT

Not long after I left evangelicalism, I was floundering. I was unsure what direction my spiritual life would take, but that didn't stop life from moving on. The world still turned, and I still had responsibilities that needed my attention.

There came a day when I could no longer ignore the fact that I needed a new laptop. Yet we didn't have money in the bank to cover the expense. I decided to pray for it. At the time, this was very unlike me. Up until this point, I had believed a prayer like this would be selfish. Praying for yourself? That you'd get something you wanted? Surely God had other things to worry about.

I wasn't sure it was something I should pray for, but I went ahead and did it anyway. I prayed for a specific amount of money to get that new laptop. I didn't discuss this matter with anyone, and there was no way anyone would know I was praying for this. Two weeks later, I walked out to bring in the mail, and there in my mailbox, to the penny, was a check for the amount I'd prayed for.

At first, it didn't compute. How in the world could I receive the exact amount of money I needed? I stood in the street, trying to absorb what was happening. I was holding in my hands the answer to one of my prayers. I'd prayed for this two weeks ago, and God had set about answering that prayer specifically for me.

It may sound silly, but this was a lesson I needed. I learned that prayer worked outside the systems, institutions, and structures. Not only that, but that I could pray for myself—for things I needed—not just for others or for "the ministry." That I mattered to God and that he was listening.

When I left the American evangelical subculture, I was scared. I'd been told that outside those spiritual systems and structures, there was only danger and death. However, I was finding that I could come to know God and rely on him and his Word. That I could know him in a real, personal, and tangible way. For the first time, I was experiencing the sufficiency of my God.

I was changing, experiencing transformation, and being renewed. Though I never would have sought the painful circumstances that sparked my journey into the desert, I couldn't deny the ways in which it was strengthening my faith.

In the past, I'd read the Scriptures primarily through the traditions of men rather than through the power of the Holy Spirit. Now that I was experiencing my Creator by faith and faith alone, rather than the interpretation of a specific denomination being at the forefront of my reading, the Spirit could reveal and fully center the truth.

My faith was being deconstructed and reconstructed in holy fire. My soul matured as never before. I stepped back from flippant certainty, unsure of what things meant, what to do, or how to handle myself in this new territory. I fully acknowledged the depth of my own lack. It was both beautiful and scary.

No wonder the wilderness has a reputation. Though hauntingly beautiful, the terrain can seem harsh and unforgiving, especially if we drop in unprepared. But when we have the right tools in our belt, we can experience a transformation of our faith unlike anything we've ever known. Like any other explorer, you will need a compass—a way to find true north. You'll need a light source—something that guides your path along your quest for truth. You'll need a map—something that outlines the routes you might follow. And you'll need a canteen—one secure enough to hold the living water to quench your soul.

Finding True North

In the wilderness, we can't just listen to any voice—any teaching—any wisdom. We need a fixed point that we can turn to for guidance no matter where we are. We need a true north.

I once talked to a woman who suffered from a recurring nightmare. She kept seeing herself perishing in hell. This woman was in a spiritual wilderness, but she had no navigation points by which to fix her compass. She was lost in the darkness, susceptible to deceiving spirits. Frightened, she called her relatives. They assured her they knew how to help. In a ritual, they laid flower petals over her body.

I asked her in what name these deeds were done.

"In the name of the ancestors," she said.

I decided to press further. "Let me ask you a question. You believe in light and darkness, right?"

"Absolutely."

"You believe in spirits?"

"Right."

"Do you believe that there could be deceiving spirits?"

She did.

At this point, I realized that what she needed was not to be convinced of the reality of the spiritual realm. What she needed was a fixed point—a true north to which she could look for spiritual guidance. What she really needed was to find God himself.

The same goes for us.

When we follow the call into the wilderness, if we're going to walk by faith and wrestle against principalities and powers, we can't just settle for anything or anyone who claims they can help. We must learn what will lead us to God—our fixed guiding point, our true north.

We need the Creator himself, who is accessed through the power of the Holy Spirit. Our access has been made possible through the person and work of Yeshua, the Light of the World.

LIGHTING YOUR PATH

When you're walking by faith, you're caught in the struggle not just between light and darkness but between greater lights and lesser lights—true spirits and deceiving spirits. There are spirits of light and darkness. How can we tell the difference? Without a way to differentiate the two, you'll find navigating the wilderness nearly impossible. There are the true sons and daughters of God, who will lead you to the Greatest Light, and there are false sons and daughters of god, who will lead you to lesser lights—themselves.

Case in point: When I first entered the Christian community in college, everything that had felt like a cultural norm up to that point in my life was stripped away. I was made to feel that I couldn't wear my hat anymore. Shouldn't wear my baggy clothes or use slang. No more fresh sneakers. Everything connected to where I came from was replaced. I was never free to be South Dallas. All of that had to go.

The only time that part of my life resurfaced was when I was being sent back into neighborhoods like mine on "missions." So I learned to code-switch, shutting the real me on and off—all for the sake of bringing people back into the fold, where they'd be changed into "new and improved" versions as well.

For a time, it felt like the way I was naturally wasn't acceptable. That everything unique about my story—everything that made me *me*—had to be flattened out in order to meet some unspoken cultural standard. I was caught by lesser lights, and to get free, I needed to remember what the apostle John said: Spirits must be tested.[4]

Lesser lights set themselves up as the pinnacle of spirituality. Rather than leading you through the wilderness, they seek to lead you off the path to populate their own little desert kingdoms. If they draw you aside, they will put you to work—for them. Whether powerful individuals or collective spiritual institutions, lesser lights all work from the same playbook.

These lesser lights position themselves as the only ones with real spiritual enlightenment, and they paint everyone outside their seeming desert oasis as heretics, heathens, and hustlers. They see their role as ushering people directly into the presence of God, but by positioning themselves as the ultimate deciders of who's right and who's wrong, they've attempted to take on the role of God himself. They gather people to themselves, not in service of the kingdom but in service of their own earthly spiritual plantations. These plantations demand the work and loyalty of the sharecroppers while enriching only those who own the land—not the One who created it.

Here's what makes the whole situation so difficult to navigate: Though lesser lights, they still position themselves as lights. Their work has an effect. They do some good. They may actually believe that they're doing the work of the Holy Spirit, laboring for the benefit of others. But when they hold people accountable to themselves and their human-made systems rather than to God and his ultimate glory, they dampen people's spiritual freedom rather than fuel it.

In the end, no man or woman is the ultimate decider of right and wrong. Only God is. When we let someone take the position of authority in our lives that only he should have, we allow others to spiritually sharecrop our souls.

For those who follow Yeshua: Your salvation is a cosmic act of God. Your Creator wrote your name in the Lamb's Book of Life and called you out of darkness. Yes, he may have used certain tools along the way—certain lesser lights to point you to himself—but make no mistake: The fate of your soul does not depend on any leader, church, or system you encounter on your journey, and your ongoing spiritual life does not depend on any person, structure, institution, or denomination. There is only one true Light of the World. He is the one you answer to, and he is the one who will light your path in the wilderness. We meet him through the power of the Spirit and the Word of God, which together act as our map, leading us through the wilderness.

FOLLOWING THE MAP

Increasingly, I'm witnessing how people who are desperate to escape a toxic culture, in their eagerness to distance themselves from a structure that harmed them, will do away with everything that reminds them of it—including core truths of their faith. Weary of didactic rhetoric, they decide that rather than sort through the information to see what should go and what should stay, they run to the other end of the spectrum, claiming they're done with "truth" and that all they need is a sense of God's Spirit. This impulse, while certainly relatable, is an overreaction. It's like getting burned with bad GPS route guidance and then throwing away all maps. The Spirit was sent to guide us in all truth. Therefore, the question isn't one or the other. We need both Spirit and truth to awaken a better us.

Early in his ministry, Yeshua talked to a woman from Samaria.

She'd come to draw water from a local well and found him there, and they started talking. When she realized she was talking to a teacher, she asked him a deeply theological question regarding where the true place for worship should be. Did God's true follow-ers worship on Mount Moriah in Jerusalem or on Mount Gerizim in Samaria?

> We need both Spirit and truth to awaken a better us.

In the way he so often did, in-stead of simply answering the sur-face question, Yeshua responded to a deeper need that the woman's initial question revealed. Instead of focusing on the location of worship, he zeroed in on the intent of the worshippers themselves. "God is spirit," he told her, "and those who worship him must wor-ship in spirit and truth."[5]

In his answer, he was showing this woman that what mattered wasn't so much *where* people worship, but *Who* they worship and *how*. Your country of origin, church of choice, or denominational home is not what centers you in faith. While those factors are important and impact your development as a Christian, they are not ultimate. What truly matters is that you worship your God in spirit and in truth.

Institutional faith, while obsessed with defending things that are "true," often misses out on *the truth*. I put the word *true* in quotes for a reason. This isn't just semantics. There really is a differ-ence, and our spiritual transformation can hinge on understanding it and taking it to heart. When we focus on what's "true," we're focusing on principles rather than people. While principles certainly do affect people, the tendency in institutional faith is to prioritize principles over people in a way that's not just counter-productive but often harmful.

In his interactions with the spiritual sharecroppers of his day,

Yeshua never settled for merely debating the finer points of the law. Instead, he always pushed the discussion deeper, highlighting why the law exists and how it should be correctly applied.

For example, during a debate about sexual ethics, Yeshua told the crowds, "You have heard that it was said, 'You shall not commit adultery.' But I say to you that everyone who looks at a woman with lustful intent has already committed adultery with her in his heart."[6] While it's true that you shouldn't commit adultery, Yeshua showed that following this simple rule wasn't enough—and, more importantly, the rule wasn't even the whole truth.

The whole truth is that sexual immorality is a symptom of a deeper disease of the heart. The real issues are more complicated than adultery. Focusing on what was merely true—that the law said not to commit adultery—would get you in good with the spiritual leaders, but it missed the issues of the heart.

When we're in institutional and spiritual bubbles, it's easier to focus on things that are "true." Why? "True" things can be taught with confident certainty. We can draw a line in the sand and check to see if people are toeing it. While "true" things can be controlled, *the truth* is, in a sense, uncontrollable. It is complex and often messy. Truth must be internalized, and once applied, it manifests itself in diverse ways.

Whenever you encounter the teaching of the Scriptures, the information you are receiving contains both what is true (that is, what can be categorized and didactically taught) and *the truth* (something unquantifiable that must be lived out situationally through the power of the Holy Spirit). Neither of these can stand alone. In fact, for scriptural principles to be applied correctly, both sides must work in harmony with one another.

As you step into the wilderness, remember this: When you learn facts, lessons, and principles from Scripture, you are learning what is true. When you apply these truths to the shape of your life, you are experiencing the truth. When you live what you know and know what you live, you are walking in truth. The ultimate example of this dynamic is Yeshua, who didn't just know truth but embodied it as the Word made flesh.[7] His example as seen in Scripture is your map to follow. When we examine our map, we see how even Yeshua needed water for his soul—especially in the wilderness.

Water Your Soul

Once I stepped into the wilderness, I felt alone. Disconnected. And I knew that wasn't good. Fortunately, I met a mentor who showed me the importance of growing in community and taking time to invest in others. He showed me how to put down the kind of roots that would keep me connected to my faith—and to others.

I began meeting with a group of men on Tuesdays at 5 A.M. We called this "the Ungodly Hour." Starting around 4:45 A.M., a line of cars would begin to build down my block. I brewed the coffee, and the men shuffled in with coffee cake or donuts. Around my cracked kitchen table, we prayed, studied the Bible, and shared with one another about what was going on in our lives.

These gatherings continued for more than thirteen years. As members of the group moved and our lives changed, we've splintered off to form other groups—other gatherings. This process proved to me that God could show up outside a church building, that being a person of faith wasn't about being a cog in the wheel or a part of a packaged program. Instead, I could be a full participant in a mutual faith community.

Together, this band of brothers matured collectively, and much of the depth I have now found its origins in that group. There was nobody over us but God. This created a sobriety and realness to our faith. We were learning to water our own spirits.

When you water your spirit, you don't spiritually self-generate. That is simply not possible. Only God can speak life into death.[8] In order to water your spirit, you must learn to hear from God for yourself. Just make sure you're not working out what you learn *by* yourself.

One of the ways we learn to water our spirits is by studying Scripture. Studying for yourself is important, but remember: Scripture was not given for private interpretation.[9] God's given us all different levels of understanding, different gifts of discernment, and complementary strengths and weaknesses. We're not meant to walk alone. We're a community. A family. That is still true even in the wilderness. Stepping out in faith doesn't mean you become a spiritual exile, going it alone with just your canteen and your Bible. Being out from under the control of human-made systems and structures doesn't mean you become a law unto yourself.

Those who try to make it on their own can easily fall prey to deceiving spirits. As you distance yourself from the systems and structures, stay connected to the saints. As you study and learn and grow, share your revelations with a faith community to ensure that you are not being deceived by lesser lights, heading down a pathway toward darkness and bondage. Share, learn, and grow in both knowledge and discernment, remembering that Spirit and truth cannot be divided.

EMBRACE THE CALL

Perhaps you're stuck surrounded by institutional faith. You feel the weight of all that's wrong, and yet you hesitate. You call it caution. You call it fear. Whatever you call it, don't let it win. Your God—who is present everywhere, powerful everywhere, and capable of meeting your needs in every way—can grant you the faith to step through the fear.

This is the same path the Israelites followed as they left Egypt. They set out knowing who their God was and where he planned to take them. They knew they were headed to the Promised Land, though they didn't know exactly where it was or how they would get there. God spoke to them through his prophet Moses, guiding them every step of the way and providing them with what they needed to thrive—literally lighting their path with fire and providing them with water. They experienced his sufficiency and followed after him in community. No, their responses to their situation weren't executed perfectly. But we see the Creator's design clearly reflected in their story. He was their true north, and he provided light for their path, a map to guide them, and provision for them to water their souls, both individually and together as a community.

We have the same opportunity and can experience the same dangers that the Israelites faced. We can stray off the path, ignore God's guidance, forsake the community, and find a million ways to try going our own way and doing our own thing. Unfortunately, as we step into the wilderness, this is exactly what many of us will do.

But remember: The call to the wilderness is not a call of devastation. It is an invitation to follow God, rely on his Word, and find community among others committed to following God faithfully. The wilderness is not our final home but our pathway to the Promised Land. Some of us will not witness the fullness of God's glory until we follow him into the wilderness and take the next steps on our journey of transformation.

TALK IT OUT

1. The call to the wilderness is an invitation, not a devastation, yet it can often feel devastating, especially initially. Why is that?
2. In what ways might answering the call to the wilderness look different for different people?
3. What practical tools can help us survive a season in a spiritual wilderness?

WORK IT OUT

Think of a time when you lost sight of God as your true north. What was the outcome?

What are some ways to keep your eyes focused on God while you're in a spiritual wilderness—particularly if you're stepping away from institutions? Write down some ideas.

Lesser lights lead us to themselves rather than to God. Write down a list of lesser lights that can lead people astray, as well as tips you might use to recognize that you've been following one.

WRITE IT OUT

We need both Spirit and truth to guide us on our journey. Spend five minutes freewriting about Spirit, truth, and life in the wilderness. How can we connect to each of them? Be sure to include a few practical ways you plan to stay connected to both Spirit and truth.

Conclusion

A Better You

Though I came into this world disadvantaged, under-resourced, and unequipped, my starting place was ultimately no hindrance to the path my Creator had prepared for me. Like he did with Moses in the wilderness, God prompted me to look down and see what was in my hands. When Moses looked down, he saw a rod. There was a time that when I looked down, all I saw were problems and losses.

But what I thought was a disqualifying story actually qualified me. All my seeming disadvantages gave me unique strengths and abilities. Nearly losing my brother all those times made me a protector. Suffering the death of my dad made me a more empathetic coach. Learning everything the hard way and building a business from the ground up empowered me to help people who feel they're genuinely starting out with nothing. All the things that I thought made me weak, disadvantaged, and insignificant were actually things God used in powerful ways to help awaken a better me.

My transformation began when I stopped allowing my circum-

> **All the things that I thought made me weak, disadvantaged, and insignificant were actually things God used in powerful ways to help awaken a better me.**

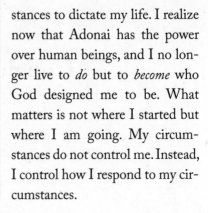

stances to dictate my life. I realize now that Adonai has the power over human beings, and I no longer live to *do* but to *become* who God designed me to be. What matters is not where I started but where I am going. My circumstances do not control me. Instead, I control how I respond to my circumstances.

RISE UP

You have the tools to transform your life. But unless you exercise your agency, you'll be stuck on the ground, like an airplane driving on the highway alongside cars, trucks, and vans. You'll putter along at a snail's pace, stuck in traffic jams and subject to all the accompanying frustrations. Friend, you were designed to fly. You have been called to soar high in the sky, lifting others up with you.

While all airplanes start on the ground, they're not meant to stay there. Runways are of limited lengths, with one purpose only: to allow airplanes to get up to speed quickly enough to start climbing through the air. A runway simply becomes a dead-end road when you don't exercise your agency. But when you exert your power and take control of your life, you'll find that it doesn't matter when the road narrows or seems less fitting. When you see the dead end approaching, you won't even blink. You'll know your time has come. It's time to fly.

FIGHT FOR YOUR FUTURE

During my own personal transformation, I learned that my attitude toward my life would make or break me. I went from passively accepting whatever was handed to me to practicing agency in my life. From hating certain aspects of who I was to realizing those very things were my secret superpowers. From needing to be uplifted to uplifting others.

Now when I see something blocking my path, whether it be a challenge or a bully, my response isn't to turn back. It's to lift my chin and square my stance. I won't back down. Instead, I'm gonna fight. You can do the same.

Transformation isn't about making a name for yourself, building a platform, or becoming a superstar. It doesn't have to be over-the-top to be real. Genuine change isn't rooted in flashes and fireworks. It's rooted in you, right now, just as your Creator made you. Remember, the goal is not to change who you are. The goal is to awaken a better you in every part of your life: mentally/emotionally, physically, relationally, and spiritually. If you haven't already started the journey using the resources in this book, then the only thing you're waiting on is you. Will you fight for your future?

Think of the areas in which you're experiencing desperation. What steps will you take to seek the right information? Who will guide you as you seek to apply what you're learning in the right way? How will your life transform as a result—mind, body, and spirit? The answers to these questions will unlock your journey to transformation. Start taking steps now, and you'll be on your way toward awakening a better you. Your life will transform—and with it, your community.

> The goal is to awaken a better you in every part of your life.

POWER AND RESPONSIBILITY

Remember sitting behind the wheel of a car for the first time? Your fingers tightly gripped the steering wheel. The thought of cranking the engine felt terrifying. The slightest error could send you spinning off the road into a fireball of chaos. That is how it feels when you finally sit in the driver's seat of your own life. You know turning the wheel will cause things to change, and that's scary. And your fear isn't just about you either—others are depending on you to control your direction and speed. What will happen to them if something goes wrong?

Perhaps you're thinking that you'd rather not have this level of responsibility. If that's the case, you'll never truly be free. Freedom isn't just about being able to go where you want, buy what you want, eat what you want, and do what you want. True freedom means no longer being controlled by anyone or anything, including your own selfish desires. Your Creator, who has authority over everything, will hold you accountable for how you live your life. The more freedom you have, the more responsibility you bear to use your power for good and help others be free.

Without this perspective, your agency can easily morph from a helpful tool to a weapon. If you don't accept responsibility for your life, you risk becoming an oppressor rather than a creator. Since you're designed in the image of the Creator, that pattern is harmful and unhealthy because it works against your ultimate design. You weren't made to hold others down. Like your Creator, you were designed to lift them up. You were designed to fly together.

FIGHT FOR OUR FUTURE

As I have grown, I've gone from not knowing how to move forward to establishing Build a Better Us, a full-scale organization that has become a leader in holistic transformation. We serve everyone from orphans, college students, and teachers to organizational leaders and aspiring writers—you name it. Our directors at BBU are powerful leaders in their own right, ones who have emerged from unsuspecting backgrounds by applying the same principles outlined in this book. Every win their clients experience is linked inextricably to their own—just as their wins are linked to mine.

When you awaken a better you, you influence the environment and the people around you, people who will benefit from your wisdom, courage, and example. When you move toward holistic health, you make the world a better place—together. We are all stronger and better together, and the greater your individual transformation, the stronger everyone grows. Transformation creates synergy, and that synergy needs a catalyst—you.

Because when you're a better you, we can all be a better us.

Acknowledgments

I want to offer my thanks to all who have helped me and poured into my life and this project.

To God, for guiding my steps and being the light in my life, even when I didn't want light or wasn't sure light was real. You illuminated my pathway and created this adventure I've been living the last forty years.

To my wife, Vanja, for being my partner, confidant, and lover. You are my backbone and my mutual support system.

To my mother, Teresa, for having me and unselfishly giving me everything you knew and all you had.

To my brother, Joe, for being my friend and companion through my whole life. We've done so much together, laughed hard, and supported each other all the way. Thank you for being my best friend.

To my "twin," Pat, for being a very good friend and brother in my life. We share personalities, and because you have such a healthy understanding of my story, you've been able to help me find clarity and recognize my strengths in ways other people couldn't.

To my sister, Rachel, thank you for being both tough and tender. You've been a resilient example above all others.

To my circle, Tedashii, Lecrae, and Adam, we are the fantastic four. For many years, you have been my emotional, spiritual, and personal support. Thank you for loving me in the darkest times and supporting me through the peaks as well. You have been steady and consistent throughout seasons and changes, and I'm grateful for you.

To my mentors, for seeing me, recognizing my potential, and helping me develop in many different aspects. Without you, I would not have had examples of what I wanted to become in terms of competence and compassion.

To all my many friends I've had throughout the years—through elementary, high school, college, and beyond. You've all meant so much along my journey. You've offered companionship, shaped my life, and helped challenge me. Together, we survived some volatile environments, and our friendship helped me become someone I didn't know I could be.

To my family, for being my rock, offering support, and setting an example of compassion. You are kind, generous, selfless, and strong. You've shown me the way.

To Theresy Yosef, thank you for being my partner. You are one of the reasons why Build a Better Us exists. Your drive and passion have influenced many aspects of the organization and who I have become as a person. This book would not be possible without you. Most of what you've done will never be seen by the world, but it is not unseen by God.

To Ruth Buchanan, my other twin. I want to thank you for helping me bring clarity to my mind and ideas in a way people can understand.

To my agent, Ingrid Beck, thank you for fighting for me and believing in me.

To the team at Penguin Random House, specifically Kimberly Von Fange and Andrew Stoddard, thank you for excellent editorial guidance. You are so sharp, and you have helped me hone my ideas and strengthen the project.

And to everyone who believed in me when all I had was potential, I thank you from the bottom of my heart. Without your love and support, this book wouldn't be possible.

Notes

PART ONE: START HERE

1. Ingrid Gould Ellen, "Welcome Neighbors? New Evidence on the Possibility of Stable Racial Integration," *Brookings*, December 1, 1997, www.brookings.edu/articles/welcome-neighbors-new-evidence-on-the-possibility-of-stable-racial-integration.

CHAPTER ONE: HIGH RISK, HIGH REWARD

1. Ruth 4:15.

CHAPTER TWO: THE VALUE OF YOU

1. Lawrence Wright, *Twins: And What They Tell Us About Who We Are* (New York: John Wiley & Sons, 1997), 5.
2. Rome Neal, "Personality Traits Linked to Birth Order," *CBS News*, June 10, 2022, www.cbsnews.com/news/personality-traits-linked-to-birth-order.
3. Kim Parker et al., "What Unites and Divides Urban, Suburban and Rural Communities," Pew Research Center, May 22, 2018, www.pewsocialtrends

.org/2018/05/22/what-unites-and-divides-urban-suburban-and-rural
-communities.

4. Romans 12:1–2.

5. Kate Jones, "Do Introverts Make Better Leaders?," *The Sydney Morning Herald,* March 6, 2014, www.smh.com.au/business/small-business/do -introverts-make-better-leaders-20140304-341fr.html.

6. Romans 12:6–8.

CHAPTER 3: ON THE RED CARPET

1. Brian A. Primack et al., "Use of Multiple Social Media Platforms and Symptoms of Depression and Anxiety: A Nationally-Representative Study Among U.S. Young Adults," abstract, *Computers in Human Behavior* 69 (April 2017): 1–9, www.sciencedirect.com/science/article/pii /S0747563216307543?via%3Dihub.

2. Jaqueline V. Hogue and Jennifer S. Mills, "The Effects of Active Social Media Engagement with Peers on Body Image in Young Women," abstract, *Body Image* 28 (March 2019): 1–5, www.sciencedirect.com/science /article/pii/S174014451730517X#!.

3. Shainna Ali, "Is Social Media Making You Lonely?," *Psychology Today,* October 5, 2018, www.psychologytoday.com/us/blog/modern-mentality /201810/is-social-media-making-you-lonely.

4. "Current World Population," Worldometer, www.worldometers.info/world -population.

5. Tony Manfred, "Kobe Bryant Says He Counts Every Single Made Shot During Shooting Practice, Stops When He Gets to 400," *Business Insider,* February 22, 2013, www.businessinsider.com/kobe-bryant-describes -shooting-practice-routine-2013-2.

6. Galatians 6:7–9.

CHAPTER 4: BEWARE THE WIZ

1. *The Wiz,* directed by Sidney Lumet, written by Joel Schumacher (Universal City, Calif.: Universal Studios, 1978), DVD.

2. Proverbs 11:14.

3. *The Wiz,* 1:27:46.

4. Matthew 5:3.

5. 1 Samuel 17:1–50.

CHAPTER 5: AWAKEN A BETTER MENTAL AND EMOTIONAL YOU

1. Bessel van der Kolk, *The Body Keeps the Score: Brain, Mind, and Body in the Healing of Trauma* (New York: Penguin, 2014), 30.

2. Van der Kolk, *Body Keeps the Score,* 46.

3. Kuljeet Singh Anand and Vikas Dhikav, "Hippocampus in Health and Disease: An Overview," *Annals of Indian Academy of Neurology* 15, no. 4 (2012): 239–46, www.ncbi.nlm.nih.gov/pmc/articles/PMC3548359.

4. Van der Kolk, *Body Keeps the Score,* 137.

5. Norman Doidge, *The Brain That Changes Itself: Stories of Personal Triumph from the Frontiers of Brain Science* (New York: Penguin, 2007), xix–xx.

6. Doidge, *Brain That Changes Itself,* 59–60.

7. Hebrews 11:17–19.

CHAPTER 6: AWAKEN A BETTER PHYSICAL YOU

1. 1 Corinthians 10:31.

2. Genesis 1:31.

3. Ashkan Afshin et al., "Health Effects of Dietary Risks in 195 Countries, 1990–2017: A Systematic Analysis for the Global Burden of Disease Study 2017," *The Lancet* 393, no. 10184 (May 2019): 1958–72, www .thelancet.com/journals/lancet/article/PIIS0140-6736(19)30041-8 /fulltext.

4. Afshin et al., "Health Effects."

CHAPTER 7: AWAKEN A BETTER RELATIONAL YOU

1. DJ Envy, Angela Yee, and Charlamagne tha God, "Lecrae Interview and More," August 26, 2020, in *The Breakfast Club,* podcast, 1:25:44, https:// podcasts.apple.com/gh/podcast/lecrae-interview-and-more/id1232428553 ?i=1000489219227.

2. Joanna Moorhead, "Let's Talk About Intimacy—and Why It Makes for Better Love and Sex," *The Guardian*, April 29, 2017, www.theguardian.com /lifeandstyle/2017/apr/29/intimacy-sex-better-relationships.

3. Chris Huber, "2017 Hurricane Harvey: Facts, FAQs, and How to Help," World Vision, www.worldvision.org/disaster-relief-news-stories/2017 -hurricane-harvey-facts.

4. Acts 2:46; 1 Corinthians 11:23–25; Jude 1:12.

5. Ecclesiastes 3:1.

CHAPTER 8: AWAKEN A BETTER SPIRITUAL YOU

1. *Black Panther*, directed by Ryan Coogler (Burbank, Calif.: Walt Disney Studios Motion Pictures, 2018).

2. Matthew 22:39, KJV.

3. Numbers 11.

4. 1 John 4:1–6.

5. John 4:24.

6. Matthew 5:27–28.

7. John 1:14.

8. Ezekiel 37:1–14.

9. 2 Peter 1:20–21.

ABOUT THE AUTHOR

Life coach, speaker, and author BJ Thompson has helped tens of thousands of individuals and couples all over the world experience personal and relational growth. BJ serves as the executive director for Build a Better Us, where his inspirational work has impacted millions of people. He has a bachelor's degree in sociology from the University of North Texas and a master's degree from Union University.

Alongside Grammy Award–winning artist Lecrae, BJ helped launch the 116 Movement—one of the most significant faith movements in recent history. He also expanded groundbreaking racial reconciliation work in Memphis, Tennessee. BJ has been featured in *Relevant Magazine, Propel, Christianity Today,* Barna Group, and other publications. He has also worked with the History Channel, the Ethics & Religious Liberty Commission, universities—both nationally and internationally—and other corporations. He and his wife, Vanja, have been married for more than twenty years and live in Atlanta with their three children.